'I wholeheartedly recommend this book for anyone interested in researching Islāmic psychology and psychotherapy. It provides a clear and accessible foundation in research methodology, including qualitative and quantitative techniques and the Maqasid Methodology. The authors' focus on applying Islāmic ethics to research is a unique and valuable perspective. This book is suitable for beginners and recommended for undergraduate and postgraduate courses.'

Zuleyha Keskin, *PhD, Course Director and Senior Lecturer at the Centre for Islāmic Studies and Civilisation, Charles Sturt University, a co-founder of ISRA Australia and the Managing Editor of the Australian Journal of Islāmic Studies, Australia*

'Professor Rassool has offered the world a timely book to guide researchers in the emerging field of Islāmic Psychology. As the director of America's first and only Islāmic Psychology research lab situated within an academic university, I look forward to recommending this book to my students and research interns who are working to further and deepen this noble field.'

Rania Awaad, *MD, Clinical Associate Professor, Stanford University School of Medicine, Director, Stanford Muslim Mental Health and Islāmic Psychology Lab, President and Co-Founder, Maristan, USA*

'G. Hussein Rassool's new book *Research Scholarship in Islāmic Psychology* provides timely and relevant research guidance to undergraduate and postgraduate students interested in Islāmic psychology. The author's reference to the Maqasid methodology is especially worthwhile due to its focus on the revealed knowledge, holism and connectivity. It is expected that this book will be instrumental in advancing the discipline of Islāmic psychology and counselling.'

Ildus Rafikov, *PhD, Director of Research, Maqasid Institute*

'Prof. G. Hussein Rassool made a successful attempt to make Islāmic psychology more accessible to modern clinical psychologists, psychotherapists and counsellors and among many others. I wish to congratulate the author for his outstanding effort in producing a work of high-quality research. It introduces Islām's holistic approach to health: physical, psychological, social, emotional and spiritual. Islāmic psychology is a development field that continues to receive much-needed attention from various contemporary scholars in the field of psychology. I believe this book to be a cornerstone contribution and therefore strongly advise it to specialist and non-specialist readers alike.'

Süleyman Derin, *PhD, Professor of Sufi Studies, Faculty of Theology, Marmara University, Istanbul, Turkey*

Integrated Research Methodologies in Islāmic Psychology

This book provides a foundation of the methodology of research scholarship in Islāmic studies, psychology and psychotherapy, offering an understanding of the concepts and techniques of Islāmic research methodology integrated with qualitative and quantitative research. Integrating Islāmic moral and epistemological values into research methodologies, the text synthesises research methodologies and approaches (empirical, rational) with Islāmic research scholarship. Chapters include a range of topics including research ethics from an Islāmic perspective, systematic methodology of research in Islāmic studies and social sciences and inductive and deductive approaches. Other questions covered include how to integrate the Qur'ân and Hadith (rules, concepts and statements) with psychological phenomena and how to write a research proposal and research paper. Each chapter includes rich case examples and relevant practical examples.

This book is ideal for researchers and students in Islāmic psychology and psychotherapy wishing to learn more about the techniques and principles of Islāmic research scholarship in the field.

G. Hussein Rassool, PhD, is Professor of Islāmic Psychology, Centre for Islāmic Studies & Civilisations, Charles Sturt University, Australia, and Professor of Islāmic Psychology and Consultant for Riphah Institute of Clinical and Professional Psychology/Centre for Islāmic Psychology, Riphah International University, Pakistan. He is series editor of Routledge's Islāmic Psychology and Psychotherapy series.

Focus Series on Islāmic Psychology
Series Editor: Professor Dr. G. Hussein Rassool,
Professor of Islāmic Psychology

About the Series

In contemporary times, there is increasing focus on the need to adapt approaches of psychology, counselling psychology and psychotherapy to accommodate the integration of spirituality and psychology. With the increasing focus on the need to meet the wholistic needs of Muslims, there was a call to adapt approaches to the understanding of behaviour and experiences from an Islāmic epistemological and ontological worldview.

The aim of the Focus Series on Islāmic psychology and psychotherapy is to introduce a range of educational, clinical and research interventions relating to Islāmic psychology and psychotherapy that are authentic, practical, concise, and based on cutting-edge research. Each volume focuses on a particular aspect of Islāmic psychology and psychotherapy, its application with a specific client group, a particular methodology or approach or a critical analysis of existing and emergent theoretical and historical ideas.

Each book in the Focus Series is written, in accessible language, with the assumption that the readers have no prior knowledge of Islāmic psychology and psychotherapy.

Advancing Islāmic Psychology Education: Knowledge Integration, Model, and Application (2023)
By G. Hussein Rassool

Integrated Research Methodologies in Islāmic Psychology (2024)
By G. Hussein Rassool

Integrated Research Methodologies in Islāmic Psychology

G. Hussein Rassool

LONDON AND NEW YORK

First published 2024
by Routledge
4 Park Square, Milton Park, Abingdon, Oxon OX14 4RN

and by Routledge
605 Third Avenue, New York, NY 10158

Routledge is an imprint of the Taylor & Francis Group, an informa business

© 2024 G. Hussein Rassool

The right of G. Hussein Rassool to be identified as author of this work has been asserted in accordance with sections 77 and 78 of the Copyright, Designs and Patents Act 1988.

All rights reserved. No part of this book may be reprinted or reproduced or utilised in any form or by any electronic, mechanical, or other means, now known or hereafter invented, including photocopying and recording, or in any information storage or retrieval system, without permission in writing from the publishers.

Trademark notice: Product or corporate names may be trademarks or registered trademarks, and are used only for identification and explanation without intent to infringe.

British Library Cataloguing-in-Publication Data
A catalogue record for this book is available from the British Library

Library of Congress Cataloging-in-Publication Data
Names: Rassool, G. Hussein, author.
Title: Integrated research methodologies in Islāmic psychology / G. Hussein Rassool.
Description: New York : Routledge, 2023. | Series: Islamic psychology and psychotherapy | Includes bibliographical references and index. |
Identifiers: LCCN 2023033479 (print) | LCCN 2023033480 (ebook) | ISBN 9781032386751 (paperback) | ISBN 9781032386720 (hardback) | ISBN 9781003346241 (ebook)
Subjects: LCSH: Islam—Psychology—Study and teaching. | Psychology—Methodology—Study and teaching.
Classification: LCC BP175 .R376 2023 (print) | LCC BP175 (ebook) | DDC 150.88/297—dc23/eng/20230803
LC record available at https://lccn.loc.gov/2023033479
LC ebook record available at https://lccn.loc.gov/2023033480

ISBN: 978-1-032-38672-0 (hbk)
ISBN: 978-1-032-38675-1 (pbk)
ISBN: 978-1-003-34624-1 (ebk)

DOI: 10.4324/9781003346241

Typeset in Times New Roman
by Apex CoVantage, LLC

Dedicated to Idrees Khattab ibn Adam Ibn Hussein Ibn Hassim Ibn Sahaduth Ibn Rosool Ibn Olee Al Mauritiusy, Isra Oya, Asiyah Maryam, Idrees Khattab, Adam Ali Hussein, Reshad Hassan, Yasmin Soraya, BeeBee Mariam, Bibi Safian & Hassim, Dr Najmul Hussein and Mohammed Ali.

Abu Hurayrah reported the Prophet Muhammad ﷺ as saying: *'If anyone pursues a path in search of knowledge, Allāh will thereby make easy for him a path to paradise; and he who is made slow by his actions will not be speeded by his genealogy'* (Sunan Abu Dâwud).

Contents

Acknowledgements		*x*
Preface		*xiii*
List of Figures		*xv*
List of Tables		*xvi*
1	Introduction to research	1
2	Philosophy and worldview in Islāmic research scholarship	20
3	Principles of Islāmic ethics: issues in conducting research	35
4	Decolonisation, epistemological bias and limitations in psychology	47
5	Integrated research methodology and research framework in Islāmic psychology	59
6	Islāmic scholarship in research: an overview of the Maqasid Methodology	72
7	Research proposal: applying the Maqasid Methodology	84
Index		*105*

Acknowledgements

All praise is due to Allāh and may the peace and blessings of Allāh be upon our Prophet Muhammad (ﷺ), his family and his companions. I would like to thank Grace McDonnell Publisher at Routledge for her valuable and constructive suggestions during the development of the proposal, and during the process of writing. To Sara Hafeez, Editorial Assistant at Routledge for her constant support in this endeavour. It is with immense gratitude that I acknowledge the acquisition of research scholarship from colleagues of the Centre for Islāmic Psychology (CIP), and the Department of Psychology, Riphah International University; and students from the Department of Psychology, International Open University, where I developed the unique and first undergraduate course in Islāmic psychology.

I am thankful to my beloved parents who taught me the value of education. I owe my gratitude to Mariam, Idrees Khattab Ibn Adam Ali Hussein Ibn Hussein Ibn Hassim Ibn Sahaduth Ibn Rosool Al Mauritiusy, Adam Ali Hussein, Reshad Hasan, Yasmin Soraya, Isra Oya, Asiyah Maryam, Nabila Akhrif, Nusaybah Burke, Musa Burke, Dr Najmul Hussein and Mohammed Ali for their unconditional love and unending inspiration.

I would like to acknowledge the contributions of my teachers who enabled me, through my own reflective practices, to understand authentic Islām, and through their guidance to follow the right path of the Creed of *Ahlus-Sunnah wa'l-Jama'ah*. Finally, whatever benefits and correctness you find within this book are out of the Grace of Allāh, and whatever mistakes you find are mine alone. I pray to Allāh to forgive me for any unintentional shortcomings regarding the contents of this book and to make this humble effort helpful and fruitful to any interested parties.

Whatever of good befalls you, it is from Allāh; and whatever of ill befalls you, it is from yourself.

[An-Nisā' (The Women) 4: 79]

Acknowledgements xi

Praise be to Allāh, we seek His help and His forgiveness. We seek refuge with Allāh from the evil of our own souls and from our bad deeds. Whomsoever Allāh guides will never be led astray, and whomsoever Allāh leaves astray, no one can guide. I bear witness that there is no god but Allāh, and I bear witness that Muhammad is His slave and Messenger (*Sunan al-Nasa'i: Kitaab al-Jumu'ah, Baab kayfiyyah al-khutbah*).

- *Fear Allāh as He should be feared and die not except in a state of Islām (as Muslims) with complete submission to Allāh.* (Ali-'Imran 3:102).[1]
- *O mankind! Be dutiful to your Lord, Who created you from a single person, and from him He created his wife, and from them both He created many men and women, and fear Allāh through Whom you demand your mutual (rights), and (do not cut the relations of) the wombs (kinship) Surely, Allāh is Ever an All-Watcher over you).* (Al-Nisā' 4:1).
- *O you who believe! Keep your duty to Allāh and fear Him and speak (always) the truth).* (Al-Aḥzāb 33:70).
- *What comes to you of good is from Allāh, but what comes to you of evil, [O man], is from yourself* (An-Nisā 4:79).

The essence of this book is based on the following notions:

- The fundamental of as a religion is based on the Oneness of God.
- The source of knowledge is based on the Qur'ān and *Hadith* (*Ahl as-Sunnah wa'l-Jamā'ah*).
- Empirical knowledge from sense perception is also a source of knowledge through the work of classical and contemporary Islāmic scholars and research.
- Islām takes a holistic approach to health: physical, psychological, social, emotional and spiritual health cannot be separated.
- Muslims have an Islāmic or Qur'ānic worldview different from the Western-oriented worldview.
- It is a sign of respect that Muslims would utter or repeat the words 'Peace and Blessing Be Upon Him' after hearing (or writing) the name of Prophet Muhammad (ﷺ).

The author and publisher would like to thank Mark Saunders, Philip Lewis and Adrian Thornhill for permission to reproduce Figure 4.1 The research onion' from p. 52. Source: Saunders MNK, Lewis P and Thornhill A (2019) *Research methods for Business Students* (8th edition) Harlow: Pearson:, p. 130. The research onion diagram is ©2018 Mark Saunders, Philip Lewis and Adrian Thornhill and is reproduced in this chapter with their written permission. In addition, we are also grateful to Jasser Auda for permission to reproduce Chart 2, p. 100, and Chart 3, p. 102. Source: Auda, J. (2021).

Re-envisioning Islāmic Scholarship: Maqasid Methodology as a New Approach. Swansea, UK: Claritas Books.

Note

1 The translations of the meanings of the verses of the Qur'ān in this book have been taken, with some changes, from Saheeh International, The Qur'ān: Arabic Text with corresponding English meanings.

Preface

The aim of the Focus Series on Islāmic psychology and psychotherapy would be to introduce a number of themes on Islāmic psychology and psychotherapy that are authentic and based on cutting-edge research and clinical practice. In addition, the Focus Series will aim to promote understanding of the issues and complexities of Islāmic psychology and psychotherapy and make it more accessible to educationalists, researchers, clinical psychologists, psychotherapists and counsellors. Research Scholarship in Islāmic Psychology is part of the Focus Series in Islāmic Psychology and Psychotherapy that examine research methodologies from an Islāmic paradigm.

Since the late-twentieth century, 'integrated research has been used in contemporary Islāmic philosophy to reconcile Islām and modernity, and to integrate Islāmic ethics and epistemological values in social sciences. Integrated research involves integrating Islāmic moral and epistemological values in research methodologies. In the context of research from an Islāmic perspective, it is the process of synthesising research methodologies and approaches (empirical, rational) with Islāmic studies methodologies. Integrated research focuses on the integration of empirical evidence (*Ilm 'aqli*) with revealed knowledge (*Ilm 'naqli*), and the synthesis of both sources of knowledge into an integrated model based on *Tawhîdic* paradigm. According to Shafii (1985) 'The task of integration is . . . rather a systematic reorientation and restructuring of the entire field of human knowledge in accordance with a new set of criteria and categories, derived from, and based on [the] Islāmic worldview' (p. 6). Thus, the essence of integrating knowledge, from an Islāmic perspective, is to bring knowledge from the different compartments and sources under one umbrella to achieve a given goal or a set of objectives.

The purpose of the book is to provide a foundation of the methodology of academic research in both Islāmic studies and psychology with an understanding of the concepts and techniques of qualitative and quantitative research, and the application of the Maqasid Methodology. This book is ideal for the beginning researcher in Islāmic psychology and psychotherapy with minimal knowledge of basic research techniques and principles. This book is recommended for use in undergraduate and post-graduate courses focusing on research methodologies in Islāmic psychology and for the novice researcher Islāmic psychology and psychotherapy.

Reference

Shafii, M. (1985). *Freedom From the Self: Sufism, Meditation, and Psychotherapy.* New York: Human Sciences Press.

Figures

1.1	Islāmic research methodologies	5
1.2	Process of research	9
1.3	Path to research question	11
2.1	Research philosophies and data collection methods	25
2.2	Research philosophy in the 'research onion'	27
2.3	Ibn Al-Haytham's philosophy on scientific research	30
4.1	Types of research bias	52
4.2	Questionable research practices in research	53
4.3	Decolonising psychology research	55
5.1	Islāmic traditions in research scholarship	60
5.2	Integrated research methodology in Islāmic psychology	61
5.3	Framework for conducting integrated research	62
5.4	Phases of undertaking research	63
6.1	Five steps of the Maqasid Methodology	75
6.2	Cycles of reflections	78
6.3	The seven elements of the Maqasid framework	79
7.1	The Maqasid Methodology	85
7.2	Mapping of framework	86
7.3	The Cycle of Islāmic Ethical Commitment	94
7.4	The theoretical and conceptual framework	96

Tables

1.1	Differences between quantitative, qualitative and integrated research questions	12
2.1	Difference between a secular researcher and an Islāmic researcher	24
3.1	Islāmic ethical criteria for research	40
3.2	Five normative legal maxims of Islāmic law	41
6.1	Limitations of Islāmic psychology scholarship	74
6.2	Seven-element perceptualisation of the framework	80

1 Introduction to research

Introduction

Research (*Bahth*) is a word that carries a general sense in the Arabic language meaning 'to seek out or investigate a thing.' It is also called '*al-Tahqiq*,' which means investigation inquiry or probing. The term 'research' in English is from a French term 'recherche,' which indicates the 'act of searching closely' for a specific person or thing. Research is referred as 'the systematic investigation into and study of materials and sources in order to establish facts and reach new conclusion' (Oxford English Dictionary). The Oxford Learner's Dictionaries defines research as 'a careful study of a subject, especially in order to discover new facts or information about it.' Another definition of research is that it is 'the diligent systematic enquiry into nature and society to validate and refine existing knowledge and to generate new knowledge' (Naidoo, 2011, p. 47).

Thus, research is a systematic process to collect and analyse information to produce new knowledge or modify existing knowledge. Research from an Islāmic perspective is broader than the notion of the acquisition of knowledge as it is an all-encompassing term focusing on theory, action and education embedded with moral and sociopolitical implications. It is becoming increasingly important for researchers to critically reflect on Western-oriented research approaches and outcomes due of its colonialist, Eurocentric and orientalist approaches. This monocultural approach to psychology research is deemed to be problematic because it fails to consider the wider political, sociocultural and religious influences on the psychosocial and mental health problems of non-Anglo-Saxon communities. The residual effects of colonialism, post-colonialism and now globalisation of knowledge mean that research with diverse ethnic groups and non-White population have produced bias-focused outcomes. Shaikh (2023) points to, in relation to the research undertaken on British Muslims in general and Muslim women, 'how Western literature reproduces certain dynamics of repressiveness and orientalisation, and the lack of meaningful growth and development in research' (p. 74).

DOI: 10.4324/9781003346241-1

2 Introduction to research

The shifting of the research paradigm from colonisation is to challenge the long-standing biases and omissions and the dominance of the Eurocentric and orientalist psychology epistemologies in research and knowledge production. This process involves a paradigm shift and a fundamental reconsideration of what kinds of research should be undertaken, the research process itself and the type of methodology to be adopted. The need to address these issues is culminated in the development of Islāmic research scholarship based on the integration of knowledge, especially the revealed and the created knowledge, that will bring balance to the wholistic and interconnected understanding of reality and truth in knowledge production. All this leads us to maintain that the Islāmic research paradigm is blind to the fundamental belief that knowledge is integrated, connected with the Creator and wholistic rather than 'an individual entity . . . may be owed by an individual' (Wilson, 2001, p. 176). The chapter aims to provide an overview of the historical context of Islāmic scientists, the status and purpose of Islāmic psychology research and the process of research.

Classification and methods

Research is often classified into different approaches such as qualitative and quantitative, and pure and applied research. Pure (basic or fundamental) and applied research are differentiated by their purpose or goal. This distinction is illustrated by Booth et al. (2003)

> We call pure research when it addresses a conceptual problem that does not bear directly on any practical situation in the world and applied research when it addresses a conceptual problem that does have practical consequences .. . . '[what] we should think' is concerned with the conceptual problem, while 'what we should do' is with the practical problem.
>
> (pp. 51–65)

Doing pure research in Islāmic psychology is to advance its knowledge base, theories, principles in the development of conceptual and theoretical framework. There is no specificity in the aim or purpose in the quest for expanding the pool of knowledge in Islāmic psychology. In addition, pure research allows psychologists to understand the relationship between behavioural variables without providing solutions to these behaviours or phenomena. However, pure research is the source of most new information about the Islāmic worldview and can act as a foundation for applied research. In contrast, applied research is undertaken to acquire new knowledge but is directed towards solving a specific and practical problem. The purpose of this type of research is usually to have client-driven or organisation-driven purpose. It is important to note that applied research studies are dependent on the generation of knowledge from pure or fundamental research. In summary, it can be

Introduction to research 3

construed that basic research is knowledge-specific while applied research is solution-specific.

There are two methods in the approach to research: inductive and deductive. Inductive research mainly focuses on building new theories or creating new knowledge by the analysis of an observed event or a phenomenon. The inductive method is a bottom-up approach and starts with specific observations and measures to arrive at some general conclusions with broader theories. It has been suggested that Muslim scholars including Al-Shatibi, Ibn Ashur and Mohammad Bakir Al-Sader defended the certainty of induction, and the latter two scholars 'added that the outcome of the induction is 'close to certainty.' They based their argument on probability' (Auda, 2021a, p. 138). In contrast, deductive research uses a top-down approach and focuses on verifying theories or verifying an observed event or phenomena. It includes a process of testing hypothesis in order to verify a theory. Inductive approaches are associated with qualitative research, and deductive methods are more commonly associated with quantitative analysis. Though there are distinctive differences between inductive and deductive approaches to research, they can be used as complementary to illuminate the findings. Thus, undertaking research in Islāmic psychology is holistic and integrated in approach. It is about investigating the anthropological, sociocultural, psychological, economic and spiritual dimensions of life and their impact on behaviour and well-being. Research method in Islāmic psychology is broadly classified as integrated, interconnected with a web of meanings and Islāmic worldview, and wholistic.

There are three different research forms, which include exploratory, descriptive and explanatory research. The focus of exploratory research is to gain a better understanding of the exact nature of the problem to enable the conduct of more in-depth research later on. The descriptive research focuses on the 'how' and 'what,' but not on the 'why.' Finally, the explanatory research focuses on the identification of the cause-and-effect relationships and deals with the 'why' of research questions. Each of the forms of research is distinctive in its use and its form will determine the type of collection of data and data analysis.

Muslim influence on the history of the scientific method

The Islāmic Renaissance (coined as Golden Age of Islām by orientalists) is traditionally dated from the eighth century to the thirteenth century (c. 786 CE–1258 CE). However, there is a debate about the period of the Islāmic Renaissance as some historians have suggested that this Golden Age occurred between the seventh century and as late as the seventeenth century. During the period, Islāmic capital cities like Baghdad (Iraq), Cairo (Egypt) and Córdoba (Spain-Andalusia) became the cultural and intellectual centres where theologians, scholars, scientists, artists, writers, philosophers, mathematicians, physicians and philosophers excelled in scholarship, experimentation and discovery. It has been reported that the library in Córdoba, the capital of Islāmic Andalusia (Spain),

> contained over 400,000 books as compared to the Cathedral libraries in Europe where the number of books did not exceed one hundred. The old building turned out to be too small for so many manuscripts, so a new one had to be built. It took six months to get all the books there.
>
> (Islamicbridge.com, 2021)

The Islāmic Caliphate was firm believers in promoting knowledge and provided a stable environment for Islāmic scholars and others to excel in scholarship. What is remarkable, in the annals of history, is

> [t]he accomplishments made by Islāmic scholars, philosophers, humanists, and scientists in all areas of the arts and humanities, the physical and social sciences, medicine, astronomy, mathematics, finance, and Islāmic and European monetary systems over a period of many centuries.
>
> (Renima et al., 2016, p. 25)

In effect, 'One who studies the Islāmic intellectual heritage realises that it is like a beacon of light in scientific research and methodology as well as of values, conduct and behaviour in research and thought' (Dar al-Iftaa Al-Missriyyah, 2022). Research endeavours at this particular enlightened period were built from an Islāmic worldview. There is the suggestion that

> [t]he Islāmic scholars developed a strong worldview built upon pure research and often investigated scientific phenomena for the sake of finding answers. However, as with modern society, much of their research was applied science, designed to hone techniques and increase the pool of knowledge in areas that improved everyday life.
>
> (Shuttleworth, 2009)

Muslim researchers have a collective duty to generate knowledge and bear the responsibility and to convey it to people, according to the injunctions of the Qur'ān and Hadīth. Imam Zarkashi stated that:

> It is a collective duty to produce books on whoever Allāh has given understanding and insight. Despite its short lifetime, the Muslim community continues to grow and develop with regard to its intellectual capabilities and knowledge is not permitted to be concealed. If writing books were abandoned, knowledge would be lost for people.

Thus, Muslim researchers should become producers of knowledge rather than consumers of knowledge. Most Muslim scholars were free to undertake pure research and their Islāmic worldview was closely tied to theology. The attitude to scientific research and its methodology is clearly expressed by the great scientist and theorist of optics Ibn-Al-Haytham (d. after 1040 CE):

> The seeker after the truth is . . . not he who studies the writings of the ancients and, following his natural disposition, puts his trust in them, but rather the one who suspects his faith in them and questions what he gathers from them, the one who submits to argument and demonstration, and not to the sayings of a human being whose nature is fraught with all kinds of imperfection and deficiency. It is thus the duty of the man who studies the writings of scientists, if learning the truth is his goal, to make himself an adversary of all that he reads, and, applying his mind to the core and margins of its content, attack it from every side. he should also suspect himself as he performs his critical examination of it, so that he may avoid falling into either.
>
> (cited in Gutas, 2020, pp. 427–428)

Muslim scientists helped in laying the foundations for an empirical, experimental and quantitative approach to scientific inquiry. The Islāmic scholars use combined methodologies in their quest for new knowledge (Figure 1.1). For example, it has been suggested that:

> the rational method (used by philosophers Ibn Sînâ, Al-Biruni); the narrative method (used in History, jurisprudence, Qur'ânic studies); the intuitive method (use in Mysticism); the common-sense method (used in Principles of jurisprudence-logical interpretation); and the combined method (use the combination of all).
>
> (Rafikov & Akhmetova, 2021)

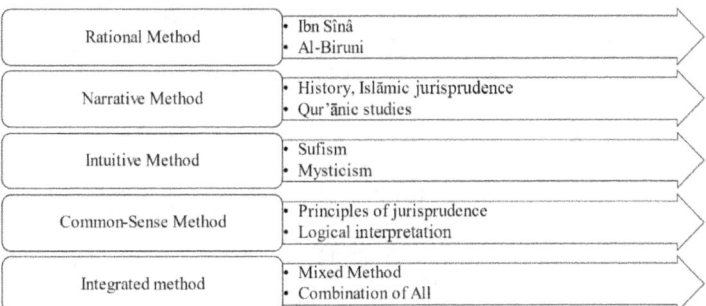

Figure 1.1 Islāmic research methodologies
Source: Adapted from Rafikov and Akhmetova (2021).

6 Introduction to research

Scholars including Abū Mūsā Jābir ibn Ḥayyān (c. 721–815 CE), often referred to as the father of chemistry, started to put a greater emphasis on the use of experiment as a source of knowledge. 'The first essential in chemistry,' he declared, 'is that you should perform practical work and conduct experiments, for he who performs not practical work nor makes experiments will never attain the least degree of mastery' (cited in Northern Kentucky University). Ibn Al-Haytham (Abū ʿAlī Al-Ḥasan Ibn Al-Haytham) (c. 965–1040 CE) made significant contributions to the principles of optics and visual perception. He was an early pioneer in the scientific method five centuries before Renaissance scientists (Gorini, 2003). He developed a scientific method that:

- States an explicit problem, based upon observation and experimentation.
- Tests or criticises a hypothesis through experimentation.
- Interprets the data and come to a conclusion, ideally using mathematics.
- Publishes the findings.

(Shuttleworth, 2009)

Al-Bīrūnī (Abū al-Rayḥān Muḥammad ibn Aḥmad Al-Bīrūnī) (c. 973–1052 CE) used participant observation in research as the first anthropologist (Ahmed, 1984). He understood 'that measuring instruments and human observers were prone to error and bias, so proposed that experiments needed replication, many times, before a "common-sense" average was possible' (Shuttleworth, 2009). Al-Ruhawi (Ishāq bin Ali al-Ruhawi) (c. 851–934 CE) was the first scholar to use a recognisable peer review process. He developed "peer review process to ensure that physicians documented their procedures and lay them open for scrutiny. Other physicians would review the processes and make a decision in cases of suspected malpractice" (Shuttleworth, 2009). Ibn Sînâ (Abu 'Ali al-Husayn Ibn Sînâ) (c. 980–1037 CE) developed a theory of experimentation (*tajriba*), criticising induction (*istiqraʿ*) as a scientific methodology. It has been suggested that Ibn Sînâ's critique of induction lead the way for a 'a theory of experimentation that have elements that are analogous to a modern conception of scientific method' (McGinnis, 2003, p. 307). The Muslim historian, philosopher and sociologist, Ibn Khaldun (Abū Zayd ʿAbd ar-Raḥmān ibn Muḥammad ibn Khaldūn al-Ḥaḍramī) (c. 1332–1406 CE) was the first pioneer to adopt a scientific approach to review the history. 'It is the science of circumstances and events and its causes are profound, thus it is an ancient, original part of wisdom and deserves to be one of its sciences' (cited in Al-Jubouri, 2005). It is reported that:

> Ibn Khaldun's method relied on criticism, observation, comparison and examination. He used scientific criticism to analyse accounts of historical events, the sources of these accounts and the techniques used by historians, examining and comparing various different accounts in order to get rid of falsifications and exaggerations and obtain some objective idea of what had actually happened.

(cited in Al-Jubouri, 2005)

Introduction to research 7

Other Islāmic scholars have contributed to the further development and refinement of research methodology. Through history, the Islāmic civilisation embraced all of these methodological schools but would utilise a particular methodology or a set of methodologies depending on the nature of the investigation. In fact, most of the classical Islāmic scholars were polymaths and being well-versed in numerous disciplines and their methodologies.

Status and purpose of Islāmic psychology research

Research plays an extremely important role in Islāmic civilisations and scholarship. Research exists to enhance society (*Ummah*) by advancing knowledge and the findings from research may be implemented through real-life applications. The utility of psychological research is undeniable. A thematic analysis was conducted by Haque et al. (2016) to identify research topical trends (the past decade) in the literature related the role of religion and spirituality in clinical practice. The following five themes were identified:

- Unification of Western psychological models with Islāmic beliefs and practices.
- Research on historical accounts of Islāmic psychology and its rebirth.
- Development of theoretical models and frameworks within Islāmic psychology.
- Development of interventions and techniques within Islāmic psychology.
- Development of assessment tools and scales normed for use with Muslims.

The authors recommended the expansion of theoretical models that are grounded in the philosophy of Islāmic thought but identified that several models may be required to accommodate different religious affiliations and levels of religiosity. Haque et al. (2016) recommended the development of clinical interventions from an Islāmic perspective, and the utilisation of Islāmic contemplative exercises such as *muraqabah*.

Since this study was undertaken, the period between 2015 and 2022, the literature on Islāmic psychology and psychotherapy has flourished with the publication of Evil eye, *Jinn* possession and mental health issues: The Islāmic perspective (Rassool, 2019); Islāmic counselling; an introduction to theory and practice (Rassool, 2016); the nature of the soul (Rothman & Coyle, 2018); integrating the Islāmic faith with modern psychotherapy (Al-Karam, 2018); the clinical application of the Traditional Islāmically Integrated Psychotherapy (TIIP) (Keshavarzi et al., 2020); Health and psychology: An Islāmic perspective. Volumes 1 and 2 (Rassool, 2020a, b); Mother of all evils: Addictive behaviours from an Islāmic perspective (Rassool, 2021a); Islāmic Psychology Around the Globe (Haque & Rothman, 2021); Islāmic psychology -Ilm An-Nafs: Tradition in human behaviour and experience from an Islāmic perspective (Rassool, 2021b); The Science of the soul (*Ilm an Nafs*): Themes in Islāmic psychology (Rassool, 2021c); Alcohol-The

8 *Introduction to research*

forbidden nectar: An Islāmic perspective (Rassool, 2022); Foundations of Islāmic psychology: From classical scholars to contemporary thinkers (Rassool & Luckman, 2022); Islāmic psychology: The Basics (Rassool, 2023a); and Advancing Islāmic psychology education: Knowledge integration, model and application (Rassool, 2023b).

The theoretical or conceptual framework of Islāmic psychology and the application of integrated psychotherapeutic techniques down to the grassroot levels remains a far cry (Rassool, 2021b). Models and approaches of Islāmic psychology are being propagated as global models despite their methodological problems, epistemological bias, misplaced epistemological certainty, lack of integrated research, the selective literature and their biased narratives and logical fallacy with 'cherry-picking.' The biggest conundrum is that after more than five decades of the 'evolution of Islāmic psychology,' there is still a dearth of educational framework and curriculum development in the integration of Islāmic ethics in psychology. How the burgeoning of courses in Islāmic psychology, psychotherapy and counselling are being developed or implemented without philosophical principles, curriculum design and development and economical with knowledge integration is beyond comprehension. Additionally, there remain limited research activities on the predictors of the effectiveness of different psychosocial interventions congruent with Islāmic beliefs and practices.

Research has several purposes: (1) refinement of the Islāmic methodology; (2) discovering new sound knowledge within Islāmic psychology; (3) verifying existing knowledge in the context of health and social, political and cultural conditions; (4) providing evidence for the efficacy of therapeutic techniques and spiritual interventions; (5) problem-solving of psychosocial issues faced by the *Ummah*; (6) and the application of the Maqasid Methodology (Auda, 2021a, 2021b) in Islāmic psychology research.

Process of research

Research involves a systematic process of data collection and analysis to find a solution to a problem. The research process is a multiple-stage, cyclic process where the stages are interlinked, in a logical process, with the other stages in the process. Each stage must be worked out sequentially and if changes are made in one stage of the process, all other stages must be reviewed that the changes are reflected throughout the process. This process is used in pure and applied research, regardless of the research methodologies. Figure 1.2 presents the stages of the research process.

Identify the problem

The first stage in the process is to identify a problem or develop a research question. This is the finding of a research problem that may be of interest to the researcher. The problem may be of a general nature which needs to be

Introduction to research 9

Figure 1.2 Process of research

narrowed. For example, if Islāmically modified cognitive therapy (CBT-IP) is your general topic of investigation. It is valuable to undertake an exploratory reading of what has already been done in the area of research. Subsequently, the specific topic could be developed. For example, the specific topics could be a study on the efficacy of Islāmically modified cognitive therapy (use a review of meta-analyses), or the clinical effectiveness of Islāmically modified cognitive therapy–based guided self-help interventions for anxiety and depressive disorders in Muslim patients. This means that the researcher should refine and narrow down the research problem in operational terms.

Review the literature

The next stage is to review the literature on the themes related to the research problem. The goals here are to obtain fundamental knowledge about the problem area in identifying the studies that have been conducted, their methodologies, their findings and their limitations. This is a long process as it requires the abstracting and indexing of academic journals, books, conference proceedings, reports, online articles etc. This is also about chasing the references as one source of referencing will lead to many others. A good library or research database will be a great help to the researcher for primary and secondary data and information sources. In the CBT-IP study, the review of literature enables the researcher to discover the magnitude of the problems of anxiety and depression in the Muslim community; the effectiveness of cognitive-behavioural therapy (CBT) with patients with depression and anxiety conditions; the limitations of CBT Muslim patients; Islāmic theory of depression; cognitive-behavioural therapy based on Islāmic principles and the examination of the effectiveness of CBT-IP in treating anxious and depressed adults, the methodologies used. The information discovered during this stage will enable the researcher to fully understand the effectiveness of CBT and CBT-IP and identify a methodological strategy to undertake the research study.

Formulating research aim(s), objectives and research questions

The next stage is the formulation of the research aim(s), objectives and research questions, which is one of the most important aspects of your study. The rationale for developing aim(s), objectives and research questions is to determine the scope, depth and the overall focus of the research study. The three elements are interconnected because it is extremely important that there is a constructive alignment aligned with each other, and that the entire research project aligns with them. The research aim is a statement that reflects the broad overarching goal(s) that needs to be achieved within the scope of the research. This is the 'what' question? The research aims for the CBT-IP study would be: This study aims to assess the effectiveness of CBT-IP with Muslim patients suffering from anxiety and depression. The research objectives are more specific and practical and are the 'how' question. This means that the research objectives are a series of steps for that the researcher needs to undertake to achieve the research aims. The objectives should be crafted on the basis of the criteria of being specific, measurable, achievable, relevant and time-bound (SMART). Let us look at some examples of research objectives based on the topic and research aims mentioned previously. Examples of the research objectives for the CBT-IP's study include:

- To examine the commonly used CBT methods used to treat anxiety and depressive disorders.
- To identify the current empirical research regarding the effectiveness of CBT in treating anxiety and depression.
- To identify the current empirical research regarding the effectiveness of CBT-IP in treating anxiety and depression in Muslim patients.
- To determine the effectiveness of CBT-IP in treating symptoms of anxiety and depression in Muslim patients.

- To assess both the immediate and long-term effectiveness of individually administered CBT-IP for the treatment of anxiety and depressive disorders.

Formulating the research questions is the next stage in the research process. The research questions are the prime focus and the driving force throughout the research process. It has been suggested that the primary importance of framing the research question is that it narrows down a broad topic of interest into a specific area of study (Creswell, 2014). The steps to developing a good research question are illustrated in Figure 1.3. However, the whole process can be somewhat iterative, where some modification of the aim and research objectives may be needed to ensure tight alignment.

The research questions are basically the research objectives transformed into question format. However, there are exceptions to this rule as some research objectives do not warrant their own research questions. The research questions should be well-aligned with the research aim and objectives. In effect, the research design and research methodology will be determined by the nature of the research questions. Research questions can be classified, depending on the type of research, into quantitative, qualitative or integrated research questions. For example, research questions that are exploratory, descriptive, contextual, evaluative and explanatory in nature will usually take the form of a qualitative approach, whereas questions that relate

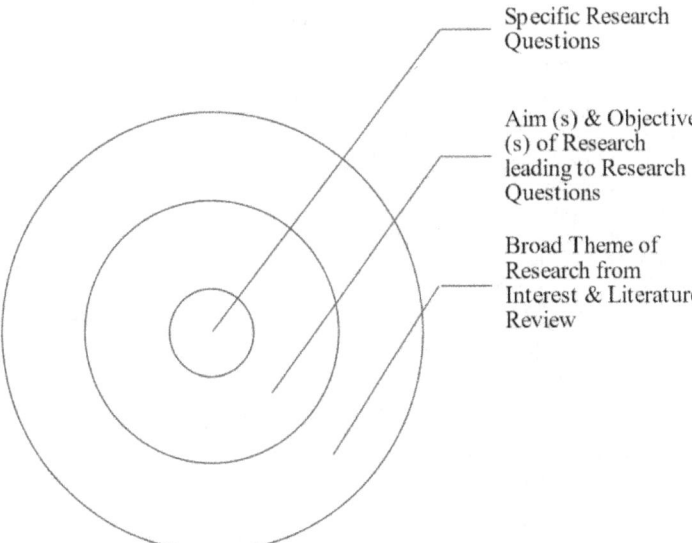

Figure 1.3 Path to research question

12 Introduction to research

Table 1.1 Differences between quantitative, qualitative and integrated research questions

Qualitative research questions	Quantitative research questions	Integrated research questions
Broad areas of research.	Sample of population to be studied, dependent and independent variables and the research design.	Use both sets of quantitative and qualitative research questions as appropriate.
Establish a link between the research question and the research design.	Establish a link between the research question and the research design. The "What" question?	
Adaptable, non-directional, and more flexible.		
Research questions: Explore, discover, identify, explain.	Descriptive research: Open-ended questions. Description of variables to measure.	
Contextual research questions seek to describe the nature of what already exists.*	Comparative research: Discover the differences between two or more groups for an outcome variable.	
Descriptive research questions attempt to describe a phenomenon.*	Relationship (association) research: Define trends and interactions between two or more variables.	
Emancipatory research questions aim to produce knowledge for the benefit of disadvantaged population.*		
Evaluative research questions assess the effectiveness of existing methods or paradigms.*		
Explanatory research questions examine reasons for and associations between what exists.*		
Generative research questions aim to provide new ideas for the development of theories and actions.*		
Ideological research questions aim to advance specific ideologies of a position.*		

Adapted from Doody Bailey (2016); * Marshall and Rossman (2014) and Ritchie et al. (2013).

to measurement or relationship or association of variables, are comparative and descriptive will make use of a quantitative approach. Table 1.1 presents the differences between quantitative, qualitative and integrated research questions.

There is great significance in the construction of the research question to ensure clarity. In order to formulate the research questions, there are a number of frameworks that can be used. One of them is the PICOT framework (Richardson et al., 1995), which is mainly used in clinical research and evidence-based studies.

- P – population, patients or problem
- I – intervention or indicator being studied
- C – comparison group
- O – outcome of interest
- T – time frame of the study

The sample research question below illustrates the PICOT framework and its elements:

Muslim adults over the age of 18 years diagnosed with anxiety or depression have better health outcomes with CBT-IP interventions compared with those with conventional CBT interventions.

P (population being studied)	Muslim adults
I (indicator or intervention)	CBT-IP
C (comparison group)	CBT
O (outcome of interest)	Decreased risk of depression or anxiety
T (time frame of interest)	Over 18 years

However, some researchers may encounter questions that are not easily adapted to the PICOT framework. An alternative for the use in qualitative research is the SPIDER (Cooke et al., 2012): Sample, Phenomenon of interest, Design, Evaluation and Research type. Another framework for use in qualitative research is SPICE: Setting, Perspective, Intervention-Interest, Comparison, and Evaluation. There are other variations of research questions framework:

PEAHEN (Population, Exposure, Adverse Health Effects, Negative reactions; as alternative to PICOC); SugABABes (Suggested Approach, Best Alternative, Best compromise; as alternative to SPICE); PEAS (Problem, Experiment, Alternative, Setting; as alternative to PIE); and SAPO (Setting, Approach, Primary Outcomes; as alternative to PICO)

(Booth, 2006)

14 *Introduction to research*

The following examples are research question based on the topic, research aim and objectives mentioned previously.

- How effective is CBT interventions with Muslim patients with anxiety and depression?
- How effective is CBT-IP interventions with Muslim patients with anxiety and depression?

In order to evaluate the research questions, the Hulley and Cummings' (2007) criteria known as the "FINER" criteria can be applied to the research questions. The FINER criteria are:

- **F – Feasible:** A good research question is feasible and realistic about the nature and scope of the research.
- **I – Interesting** not only to both researcher but also to their peers.
- **N – Novel** in bringing new insights to the field of study.
- **E – Ethical** in the implementation of the research.
- **R – Relevant** to the discipline and to the public's interest.

Formulating hypothesis(es)

Formulating a research hypothesis is supported by a good research question and will influence the type of research design for the study. The importance of formulating a hypothesis in psychology research is to provide the focal point for the research study and to provide an answer to the research question(s). To be more specific, the hypothesis indicates what and how a variable is going to be investigated in the research. There are different types of hypotheses: null hypothesis, alternative hypothesis (non-directional, two-tailed hypothesis) and directional hypothesis (one-tailed hypothesis). A non-directional hypothesis is a hypothesis with no clear direction but predicts there will be a relationship but does not specify what type of relationship. A directional hypothesis has a clear direction, predicting the findings and the type of relationship.

Examples of the various types of hypotheses in research:

- A null hypothesis: There will be no observed difference in health outcomes between interventions using conventional CBT and CBT-IP.
- An alternative hypothesis: There will be an observed difference in health outcomes between interventions using conventional CBT and CBT-IP.
- A directional, alternative hypothesis: Muslim patients with anxiety and depression who receive interventions using CBT-IP will have more positive health outcomes than those receiving conventional CBT interventions

In order to reach the final version of defining the hypothesis, there may have been several attempts and revisions during the research process.

Research design

The next stage after the formulation of the hypothesis is the research design. This is the framework of research methods and techniques identified by the researcher to conduct the study. Within both qualitative and quantitative approaches, there are several types of research design to choose from. The quantitative designs can be split into four main types: experimental and quasi-experimental designs (testing cause-and-effect relationships); descriptive and correlational designs (measure variables and describe relationships). The qualitative designs can be split into case study, ethnography, grounded theory and phenomenology designs. The types of qualitative design often have similar approaches in terms of data collection but focus on different aspects during data analysis. Each type of research designs provides a framework for the overall focus of the research methodology. The characteristics of research design include the criteria of neutrality, free from epistemological bias, being reliable and valid, and can be generalised. The outcome of the design to be applicable to a population and not just a restricted sample is an important issue in research design. A generalised design implies that the study can be undertaken with any population with similar accuracy. However, the issue of generalisation is more controversial in qualitative research. It has been argued that

> [t]he goal of most qualitative studies is not to generalise but rather to provide a rich, contextualised understanding of some aspect of human experience through the intensive study of particular cases. Yet, in an environment where evidence for improving practice is held in high esteem, generalization in relation to knowledge claims merits careful attention by both qualitative and quantitative researchers.
> (Polit & Beck, 2010, p. 1451)

Research method

Research method is the procedure of the practical 'how' of the study. This procedure involves selecting the data collection methods, collecting the primary data and analysing the data. Leedy and Ormrod (2014) provide some suggestions for what the researcher does at this stage in the research process. The researcher collects data that potentially relate to the problem; arranges the data into a logical organisational structure; analyses and interprets the data to determine their meaning; determines if the data resolve the research problem or not; and determines if the data support the hypothesis or not. The decision that needs to be taken is what type of data that need to be collected in order to answer the research questions. The sampling design is who to collect the data from. The two main categories of sampling design are probability sampling and non-probability sampling. What data to collect is important here depending on whether it will take the form of qualitative or quantitative data or both. The collection of data will use the primary or secondary source or both and whether the measurement will be descriptive or experimental. Data may be collected by experiment, observation, personal interview, telephone interviews, focus groups, literature review, meta-analyses, survey, case study, design thinking methods (brainstorming with participants to generate unique ideas or solutions), etc. The researcher should select one of these methods of data collection in the context of nature and scope of study, of resources and time frame and of the desired degree of accuracy.

For the analysis of the data, inferential statistical analysis methods to test relationships between variables, descriptive and meta-analysis, are indicated for quantitative data. For qualitative data, methods that can be used include content analysis, narrative analysis, discourse analysis, conversational analysis, grounded theory and thematic analysis. There are several programmes that quantitative research scientists can use. Statistical Package for Social Science (SPSS) is the most popular quantitative analysis software programme for both descriptive and inferential statistics, but a licence is needed. There are other software programmes, including JMP, Stata, SAS, R and MATLAB, and some of them are free to use. NVivo, ATLAS.ti, Provalis Research Text Analytics Software, Quirkos, MAXQDA, Dedoose, Raven's Eye, Qiqqa, we-bQDA, HyperRESEARCH, Transana, F4analyse, Annotations and Datagrav are some of the free research qualitative data analysis software. Hypothesis testing is a formal procedure for the statistical analysis of the research study. It is important to perform the appropriate statistical tests, and the findings from the tests will determine whether to reject or accept the null hypothesis.

Discussion

This is the penultimate stage of the research process. A useful framework is the model of description, analysis and synthesis. For presentation purpose, it would be valuable to begin with a cogent, one-paragraph summary of the study's key findings. It is important that all possible explanations and interpretations are provided for the findings of the study. Highlight how the findings of the study relate to the expectations of the study and to the literature. The findings should be examined critically in relation to how they consistently fit in or differ with knowledge about the theme. There is also a process of interpretation of the findings and the discussion of any conflicting explanations of the findings. This section should also address the limitations and weaknesses inherent in the research study. A brief overview of the implications of the findings may be required, followed by the recommendation of future or follow-up research studies. The following is a typical format used in the presentation of the research: Introduction and context of study, literature review, research methodology, findings, conclusion, recommendations, references and appendix.

References

Ahmed, A. S. (1984). Al-Beruni: The first anthropologist. *Royal Anthropological Institute of Great Britain and Ireland*, 60, 9–10.
Al-Jubouri, I. M. N. (2005). *Ibn Khaldun and the Philosophy of History*. Retrieved from https://philosophynow.org/issues/50/Ibn_Khaldun_and_the_Philosophy_of_His tory#:~:text=Ibn%20Khaldun%20went%20further%20to%20criticise%20other%20 historians,more%20closely%20akin%20to%20the%20arts%20and%20literature.
Al-Karam, C. Y. (2018). *Islāmically Integrated Psychotherapy: Uniting Faith and Professional Practice*. Conhsohocken, PA: Templeton Press.
Auda, J. (2021a). *Re-envisioning Islāmic Scholarship: Maqasid Methodology as a New Approach*. Swansea: Claritas Publishing House.
Auda, J. (2021b). The Maqasid Methodology: A guide for the researcher in the research network. *Journal of Contemporary Maqasid Studies*, 1(1), 1–30. https://doi.org/10.52100/jcms.v1i1.59.
Booth, A. (2006). Beyond PICO: The SPIDER Tool for Qualitative Evidence Synthesis. *Qualitative Health Research*, 16(10), 1283–1291.
Booth, W. C., Colomb, G. G., & Williams, J. M. (2003). *The Craft of Research*. Chicago: University of Chicago Press.
Creswell, J. W. (2014). *Educational Research: Planning, Conducting, and Evaluating Quantitative and Qualitative Research* (5th ed.). Upper Saddle River, NJ: Pearson Education.
Dar al-Iftaa Al-Missriyyah. (2022). *The Research Methodology in Traditional Islāmic Scholarship*. Retrieved October 30, 2022, from http://eng.dar-alifta.org/foreign/ViewArticle.aspx?ID=113
Doody, O., & Bailey, M. E. (2016). Setting a research question, aim, and objective. *Nurse Researcher*, 23(4). https://journals.rcni.com/doi/pdfplus/10.7748/nr.23.4.19.s5.
Gorini, R. (2003). Al-Haytham the man of experience. First steps in the science of vision. *Journal of the International Society for the History of Islāmic Medicine*, 2(4), 53–55.
Gutas, D. (2020). Alternative facts, alternative sciences: The development of the concept in medieval Islam and its historical consequences. *The Historical Review/La Revue Historique*, 17, 423–432. https://doi.org/10.12681/hr.27085.
Haque, A., Khan, F. H., Keshavarzi, H., & Rothman, A. (2016). Integrating Islāmic traditions in modern psychology: Research trends in last ten years. *Journal of Muslim Mental Health*, 10(1),75–100.
Haque, A., & Rothman, A. (2021). *Islāmic Psychology Around the Globe*. Seattle, WA: International Association of Islāmic Psychology.
Hulley, S. B., & Cummings, S. R. (2007). Conceiving the research question. In S. B. Hulley, S. R. Cummings, W. S. Browner, D. Grady, N. Hearst, & T. B. Newman (Eds.), *Designing Clinical Research* (pp. 17–25). Baltimore: Williams & Wilkins.
Imam Zarkashi. Cited in Dar al-Iftaa Al-Missriyyah. (2022). *The Research Methodology in Traditional Islāmic Scholarship*. Retrieved from http://eng.dar-alifta.org/foreign/ViewArticle.aspx?ID=113.
Islamicbridge.com. (2021). *The Lost Library of Cordoba*. Retrieved from https://islamicbridge.com/2021/10/the-lost-library-of-cordoba/.
Keshavarzi, H., Khan, F., Ali, B., & Awaad, R. (2020). *Applying Islāmic Principles to Clinical Mental Health Care: Traditional Islāmically Integrated Psychotherapy*. New York: Routledge.

Leedy, P. D., & Ormrod, J. E. (2014). *Practical Research: Planning and Design* (11th ed.). Harlow, Essex: Pearson.
Marshall, C., & Rossman, G. B. (2014). *Designing Qualitative Research*. Thousand Oaks, CA: Sage Publications.
McGinnis, J. (2003). Scientific methodologies in medieval Islam. *Journal of the History of Philosophy*, 41(3), 307–327.
Naidoo, N. (2011). What is research? A conceptual understanding. *African Journal of Emergency Medicine*, 1(1), 47–48.
Northern Kentucky University. *Jābir ibn Ḥayyān*. Retrieved from https://inside.nku.edu/artsci/departments/chemistry/about/diversity/jabiribnhayyan.html#:~:text=Jabir%20%28known%20as%20Geber%20in%20western%20history%29%20is,from%20superstition%20and%20turn%20it%20into%20a%20science.
Oxford English Dictionary. *Research*. Retrieved from https://languages.oup.com/research/oxford-english-dictionary/.
Oxford Learner's Dictionaries. *Research*. Retrieved from www.oxfordlearnersdictionaries.com/definition/academic/research1.
Polit, D. F., & Beck, C. T. (2010). Generalization in quantitative and qualitative research: Myths and strategies. *International Journal of Nursing Studies*, 47(11), 1451–1458.
Rafikov, I., & Akhmetova, E. (2021). *Methodology of Scientific Research and Concept Formation ITKI 6001*. Institute of Integrated Knowledge.
Rassool, G. H. (2016). *Islāmic Counselling: An Introduction to Theory and Practice*. Hove, East Sussex: Routledge.
Rassool, G. H. (2019). *Evil Eye, Jinn Possession, and Mental Health Issues: The Islāmic Perspective*. Oxford: Routledge.
Rassool, G. H. (2020a). *Health and Psychology: An Islāmic Perspective* (Vol. 1). London: Islāmic Psychology Publication (IIP). Amazon/Kindle.
Rassool, G. H. (2020b). *Health and Psychology: An Islāmic Perspective* (Vol. 2). London: Islāmic Psychology Publication (IIP). Amazon/Kindle.
Rassool, G. H. (2021a). *Mother of All Evils: Addictive Behaviours From an Islāmic Perspective*. London: Islāmic Psychology Publication (IIP) & Institute of Islāmic Psychology Research (RIIPR). Amazon/Kindle.
Rassool, G. H. (2021b). *Islāmic Psychology -Ilm An-Nafs: Tradition in Human Behaviour and Experience From an Islāmic Perspective*. Oxford: Routledge.
Rassool, G. H. (2021c). *The Science of the Soul (Ilm an Nafs): Themes in Islāmic Psychology*. London: Islāmic Psychology Publication (IIP) & Institute of Islāmic Psychology Research (RIIPR). Amazon/Kindle.
Rassool, G. H. (2022). *Alcohol-The Forbidden Nectar: An Islāmic Perspective*. London: Islāmic Psychology Publication (IIP) & Institute of Islāmic Psychology Research (RIIPR). Amazon/Kindle.
Rassool, G. H. (2023a). *Islāmic Psychology: The Basics*. Oxford: Routledge.
Rassool, G. H. (2023b). *Advancing Islāmic Psychology Education: Model, Application, and Implementation*. Oxford: Routledge.
Rassool, G. H., & Luckman, M. (2022). *Foundations of Islāmic Psychology: From Classical Scholars to Contemporary Thinkers*. Oxford: Routledge.
Renima, A., Tiliouine, H., & Estes, R. J. (2016). The Islāmic golden age: A story of the Triumph of the Islāmic civilization. In H. Tiliouine & R. Estes (Eds.), *The State of*

Social Progress of Islāmic Societies. International Handbooks of Quality-of-Life. Cham: Springer.

Richardson, W. S., Wilson, M. C., Nishikawa, J., & Hayward, R. S. (1995). The wellbuilt clinical question: A key to evidence-based decisions. *American College of Physicians Journal Club,* 123(3), A12–A13.

Ritchie, J., Lewis, J., Nicholls, C. M., & Ormston, R. (Eds.). (2013). *Qualitative Research Practice: A Guide for Social Science Students and Researchers.* Thousand Oaks, CA: Sage Publications.

Rothman, A., & Coyle, A. (2018). Toward a framework for Islāmic psychology and psychotherapy: An Islāmic model of the soul. *Journal of Religion and Health,* 57(5), 1731–1744.

Shaikh, A. (2023). Relevance of research methodologies used in health psychology for British Muslims: An epistemological critique on the colonisation of knowledge production. In S. Dogra (Eds.), *British Muslims, Ethnicity and Health Inequalities.* Edinburgh: Edinburgh University Press.

Shuttleworth, M. (2009). *History of the Scientific Method.* Explorable.com. Retrieved from https://explorable.com/history-of-the-scientific-method.

Wilson, S. (2001). What is an indigenous research methodology? *Canadian Journal of Native Education,* 25(2), 175–179.

2 Philosophy and worldview in Islāmic research scholarship

Introduction

The Islāmic research scholarship is based on the contributions of seminal works of classical Muslim scholars to the advancement of the principles and foundations of scientific theories and methodologies. The word 'tradition' literally means to transmit to hand over or to deliver and is translated into Arabic as *taqlid*. It is

> a belief or behaviour passed down within a group or society with symbolic meaning or special significance with origins in the past. They signify modes of thought and behaviour followed by a particular people continuously from generation to generation.
>
> (Omer, 2016)

It has been suggested that the Islāmic tradition refers to two things: intellectual production and historical reality (Dar al-Ifta Al-Missriyyah, 2022). The intellectual production is twofold. It focuses on the Qur'ān and the *Sunnah* as the primary fundamental sources of knowledge. The other focus is that '[i]ntellectual production is that which comes about from humans interacting with these two sources via worldviews, thoughts, sciences, methodologies, judgments and practices' (Dar al-Ifta Al-Missriyyah, 2022).

In contrast, the explanation accorded to historical reality

> is made up of five realms: things, people, symbols, ideas, and events. The traditional scholar would be zealous to maintain an intellectual engagement with these worlds within the context and authority of the text. That is to say, in confirming that the text is the basis of civilisation, he kept it before him when interacting with these five worlds.
>
> (Dar al-Ifta Al-Missriyyah, 2022)

For example, the classical Muslim scholar in their pursuit of knowledge did not divorce their intellectual discourse from Islāmic ethical and moral

DOI: 10.4324/9781003346241-2

values. The chapter focuses on providing an understanding of the Muslim researcher and examine their philosophical orientation. In addition, Ibn Al-Haytham's philosophy on scientific research is examined.

Understanding the Muslim researcher

It is from the rich philosophy and worldview of the Muslim researcher that we can extract the many research concepts, processes and methodologies, which form part of the Islāmic traditions based on the Qur'ānic or Islāmic paradigm. It has been suggested that '[t]he methodologies of the Islāmic tradition are crucial as a paradigm by which to understand the way in which the Muslim scholars proceeded in a variety of sciences and fields' (Dar al-Ifta Al-Missriyyah, 2022). However, the Muslim researcher in the field of Islāmic psychology and psychotherapy needs to acquire the necessary knowledge, tools and developing skills from the existing research Islāmic traditions. It

> is incumbent on us to understand what we may call the 'Islāmic paradigm.' What are its landmark signs? And how may we reformulate this paradigm such that it is amenable to a worthwhile dialogue with others? This latter is something of which are in dire need in this time.
>
> (Dar al-Ifta Al-Missriyyah, 2022)

In addition to the acquisition of '*ilm* (knowledge) and tools of research in the Islāmic traditions, the Muslim scholar's worldview and philosophical stance need to be part of this equation. Does the Muslim scholar's worldview and philosophical stance are congruent with Islāmic beliefs and practices? The Muslim scholars who have been acculturated and embedded the Islāmic paradigm in their philosophy and worldview are immune to the problems of the secular philosophical research paradigm.

The need to understand the epistemology, ontology and source of Islāmic knowledge is of paramount importance. How do the Qur'ān and the *Sunnah* form the basis of the sources of knowledge and Islāmic research? The sources of knowledge in Islām are from the Qur'ān and *Sunnah (ilm 'naqli)*, and from rational knowledge based on human intellect ('*akl*), observation and empirical (*ilm 'aqli*). It has been suggested that '[t]he systematic integration of the sources and means of knowledge into a synthesised approach is known as epistemological [relating to theory of knowledge] integration (*al-takamul al-ma'arifi*)' (Rassool, 2023, p. 62). The foundation of knowledge is the Qur'ān which

> is viewed as the springhead of all knowledge and all sciences, not because it contains the knowledge itself but, rather, because it inspires the Muslim to develop a distinctive vision of the unity among the various spheres of knowledge. The notion of this unity arises out of an awareness of the

unity of the Divine and its applications to the various spheres of human knowledge.

(Malkawi, 2014, p. 20)

In addition to the sources of knowledge from the Qur'ān, there is also the *Hādīth*. A *Hādīth* refers to the actions, statements or tacit approvals of Prophet Muhammad. From the Ḥādīth, we learn about the *Sunnah*, which is the practice of the Messenger of Allāh. It is divine revelation from Allāh and the *Sunnah* of Prophet Muhammad that become the primary and most fundamental sources of knowledge. Utz (2011) suggested that

> It is only through revelation that we can comprehend the true nature of the soul and the unseen world and ascertain the methods for purifying the soul and developing it to its fullest potential. Allāh is the only One with authentic and complete knowledge of the unseen world, so we turn only to Him for this understanding. Human beings, especially Muslims, must not speculate or guess in relation to this domain.

(pp. 39–40)

Knowledge is also gained from sense perception, intuition and rationalism (logical reasoning) and these sources should not be neglected. However, there is absolutely no contradiction between transmitted, divine knowledge from the Qur'ān and the *Sunnah* and the rational, empirical knowledge as both approaches are from the same source, that is, God, the Almighty. For the Islāmic researcher, empirical evidence should be judged and evaluated according to the criteria of the Divine revelation, and they should make an attempt to put Islāmic ethical considerations before rationality, and empirical evidence, as the latter should become secondary to the primary sources. Malkawi (2014) suggested that the classical Muslim scholars, despite their different school of thought, agreed that

> knowledge should be interconnected, complementary, and organically linked to the knowledge of God. In the view of these scholars, the fact that all sciences originate from a single divine source is the foundation for the ultimate integration and unity of knowledge.

(p. 12)

It is worth taking into consideration the importance of the Arabic language and linguistics because of the degree to which classical Muslims scholars placed emphasis on the issue of the meanings of words in the Islāmic traditions. Sadar (n.d.) (cited in Foundation for Science, Technology and Civilisation, 2006) notes that

> Scientists are accountable to God for their activities, they are required both to serve the community and to protect and promote its ethical and moral

institutions. The way they use science, therefore, must reflect the values of the society they seek to serve. Thus, the Qur'ānic approach to science is at once dynamic and static: it promotes reason, objectivity and the pursuit of truth and excellence, but at the same time, it places this endeavour firmly within the boundaries of Islāmic ethics and values.

From a historical perspective, Muslim scholars always began with the formula 'In the name of God, the Merciful, the Compassionate,' and with salutation to the Prophet. Those scholars developed their ideas, theories and methodologies from an interaction of the divine texts and empirical evidence and quoted from the Qur'ān and *Sunnah*, if relevant and appropriate. Bucaille (2000) provides us a reminder of the Islāmic traditions where

> [m]en were more steeped in the religious spirit than they are today; but in the Islāmic world, this did not prevent them from being both believers and scientists. Science was the twin of religion and it should never have ceased to be so.
>
> (p. 85)

The differences between a secular researcher and a Muslim researcher in relation to orientation, reality, research philosophy, worldview, focus, religious relationship, sources of knowledge, values, ethics, process and relationship between mind and body are presented in Table 2.1.

Philosophical orientation of the researcher

The nature and process of research are determined and conducted within a specific theoretical framework of research and this is referred to as the research paradigm based on a philosophical perspective. According to Cohen et al. (2017), the scientific research paradigm can be defined 'as a wide structure encompassing perception, beliefs, and awareness of different theories and practices used to carry out scientific research' (p. 657). The research paradigm is based on particular sets of theoretical assumptions: epistemology, ontology, methodology (Guba & Lincoln, 1994) and axiology (Heron & Reason, 1997). Epistemology is the study of knowledge and justification and seeks to address the question 'How can we find reality?' Ontology refers to the form and nature of reality and seeks to address the question 'What is true and real?' Methodology refers to approaches to defining a research question and methods and seeks to address the question 'What procedure can we use to obtain knowledge?' Axiology refers to the role of values and ethics within the research process and the values or ethical behaviour of the researcher informs the choice of methods. The assumptions we make, according to Saunders et al. (2015), are about 'human knowledge (epistemological assumptions), about the realities you encounter in your research (ontological assumptions)

24 Philosophy and worldview in Islāmic research scholarship

Table 2.1 Differences between a secular researcher and an Islāmic researcher

	Secular researcher	Muslim researcher
Orientation	Secular or Judeo-Christian	Islāmic
Reality	Objective reality does not exist	Objective reality exists
Research philosophy	Positivist or the interpretivist or critical theoretical paradigms	Holistic paradigm: Positivist, the interpretivist and the critical theoretical paradigms combined with Islāmic worldview (Qur'ānic)
Worldview	Naturalistic	Islāmic
Focus	Limited to the physical world. Disregard for spiritual dimensions	Seen and unseen world
Religious relationship	Oppositional Secular	Integrated
Sources of knowledge	Man-made theories, empirical, parochial, a posteriori judgements	Divine revelation (Qur'ān and *Sunnah*); empirical
Values	Individualism; materialistic; sociomoral value structure;value laden and dependent	Collectivism; God-consciousness; spiritual–divine will; Islāmic values and morality
Ethics	Personal experience and social culture	Qur'ān and Hādīth
Process	Individual-based and focused	Mutual responsibility. Social obligation. Healthy altruism
Relationship between mind and body	Mind–body interaction	Mind–body–soul interaction

and the extent and ways your own values influence your research process (axiological assumptions)' (p. 124).

There are two foundational paradigms in the social sciences (positivist–quantitative research and interpretivist–qualitative research), but there are several other paradigms that emerged from the foundational paradigms. Most quantitative research uses positivism as a conceptual framework for research and relies on quantitative scientific experiments of cause and effect to arrive at the 'truth' based on observable and measurable facts. It has been suggested that '[p]ositivism relates to the philosophical stance of the natural scientist and entails working with an observable social reality to produce law-like generalisations' (Saunders et al., 2015, p. 135). The interpretivist paradigm uses qualitative and, if appropriate, quantitative methods. The interpretivist approach 'emphasises that humans are different from physical phenomena because they create meanings. Interpretivists study these meanings' (Saunders et al., 2015, p. 140). This means that the researcher may have multiple

Philosophy and worldview in Islāmic research scholarship 25

interpretations of these meanings depending on the researcher's perceptions and worldviews. The pragmatism paradigm may use a combination of both the positivist and interpretivist approaches within a single study. The rationale of this approach is to identify the research methods or techniques that contribute to the most productive answer to the research problem. The methods used include ethnography, grounded theory, phenomenology, discourse analysis, heuristic inquiry, action research, etc. Realism research philosophy relies on the idea of independence of reality from the human senses. In order to understand the reality of the world, Saunders et al. (2015) suggest that

> [c]ritical realism claims there are two steps to understanding the world. First, there are the sensations and events we experience. Second, there is the mental processing that goes on sometime after the experience, when we 'reason backwards' from our experiences to the underlying reality that might have caused them.
>
> (p. 139)

The methods of research include critical discourse analysis, action research, and critical ethnography. Figure 2.1 presents the research philosophies and data collection methods.

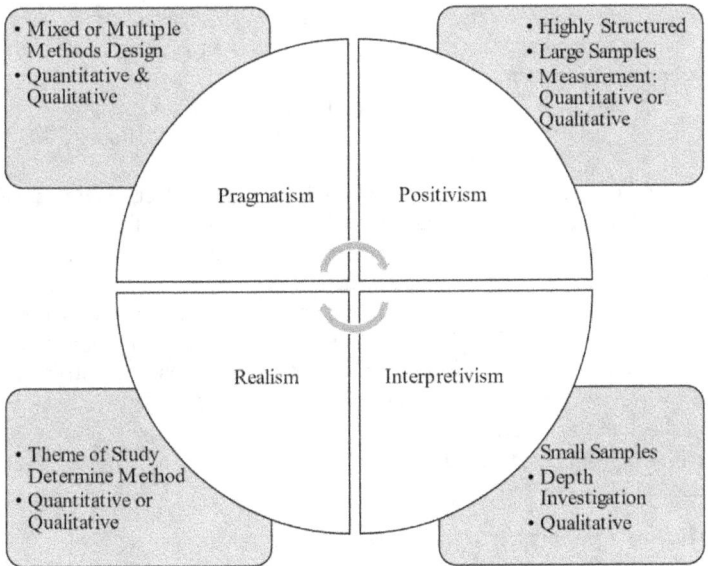

Figure 2.1 Research philosophies and data collection methods

Research philosophy and worldview

The term paradigm may also be used to describe a researcher's worldview. Worldview or paradigm refers to 'how the researcher views the world and goes about conducting research' (Creswell & Plano Clark, 2007, p. 21). Though, the terms philosophy and worldview are used interchangeably, they are two different words that convey different meanings. Philosophy 'is the study of the fundamental nature of knowledge, reality, and existence. It is characterised by a questioning approach to life and a critical examination of ethical and moral issues' (Hassan, n.d.). In contrast, worldview is composed of 'beliefs, values and assumptions, derived from the socialisation process in a specific cultural context'(Ibrahim & Kahn, 1987, p. 164). Philosophy is a broader term having a generalised picture of the world and the place of man in it, whereas worldview has the notion of perspective and is more restrictive. However, worldview is indicative of a person's philosophy. Abi-Hashem (2017) suggested that "[w]orldviews represent our pragmatic framework on existence and shapes our beliefs, attitudes, actions, and philosophies.' This means that the worldview is a set of parameters that include a wide range of fundamental matters including philosophy, themes, values, emotions, ethics, language, culture and religion. It is a subjective way of thinking and having a vision about, and interacting with, our world.

The philosophical position of a researcher is related to

> a system of the researcher's worldview, aims, thought, following which new, reliable knowledge about the research object is obtained. It is the basis of the research, which involves the choice of research strategy, formulation of the problem, data collection, processing, and analysis.
>
> (Akhmatova & Rafikov, 2021)

This means that the philosophical research paradigm reflects the researcher's assumptions and beliefs about knowledge and method that epitomises the approach of the researcher's worldview. For example, a Western scientist's paradigm of research would be determined by the scientist's worldview: positivism (or post-positivism), interpretivism, realism and pragmatism, and these need to be identified because of their influence on the nature and process of research. In essence, addressing research philosophy and integrating the worldview involved the formulation of assumptions, beliefs and values. The identification of research philosophy is positioned at the outer layer of the 'research onion' as presented in Figure 2.2.

Muslim's researcher: Islāmic worldview

The Muslim researcher's philosophical position is based on the Islāmic worldview (*Tasawur or Ru'yah al-Islām li al-Wujud*), which is based on a system of

Philosophy and worldview in Islāmic research scholarship 27

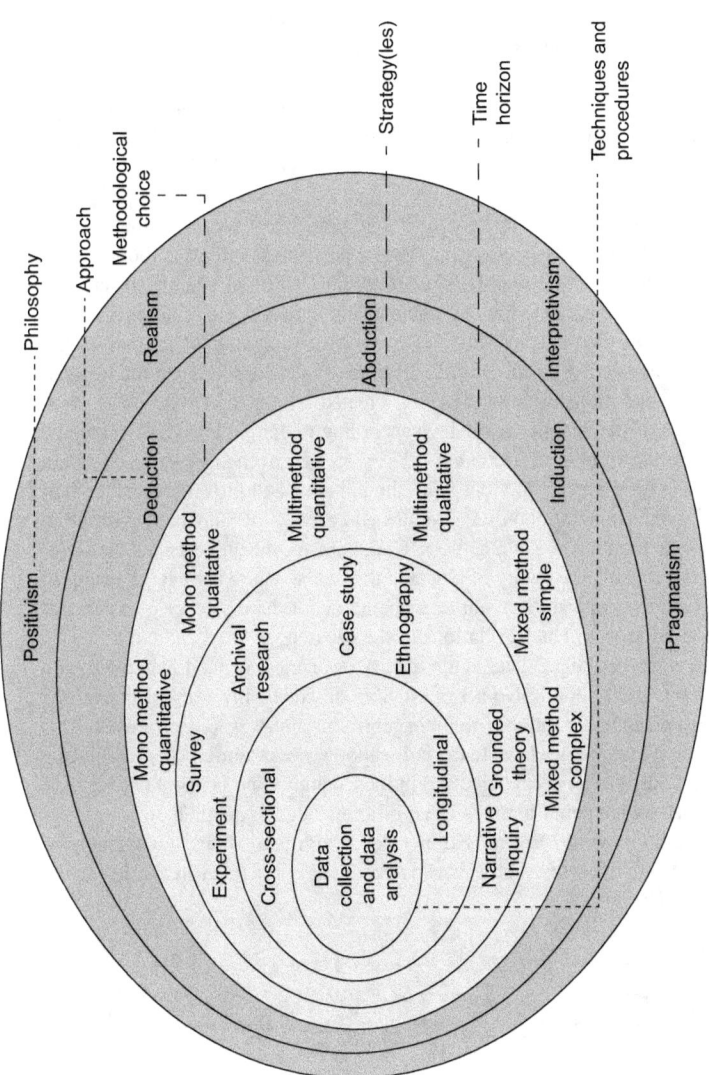

Figure 2.2 Research philosophy in the 'research onion.'
Source: Saunders et al. (2019). Permission from authors.

values and principles, derived from the Qur'ān and *Sunnah*, and the Islāmic civilisation. Islāmic worldview is identical to the Qur'ānic worldview:

> The Qur'ānic worldview is the Islāmic worldview, which determines and governs this [Islāmic] way of thinking with its related principles, concepts, and values – as well as the goals and higher aims which they seek to fulfil. This worldview should be reflected in a cogent, coherent, scientific manner in the structure of an Islāmic society's way of thinking, as well as in the ways in which this way of thinking is applied and the outcomes to which it leads.
> (Abu Sulayman, 2011, p. 2)

Abu Sulayman suggests that the Qur'ānic worldview serves as the foundation of the Islāmic perspective, guiding its principles, values, and objectives. It should be evident in both the structured thinking of an Islāmic society and its practical applications, shaping outcomes in a logical and scientific manner. Moreover, the Qur'ānic worldview 'is an ethical, monotheistic, purposeful, positive perspective on the world and those in it which reflects the healthy, well-balanced human nature that God created within us' (p. 30). The characteristics of the Islāmic worldview, according to Taqiyuddin (2020), include its derivation from God (*Rabbaniy*); *Sharīʿah* axis of the revelation of Allāh; comprehensive aspects of God, man, the universe and the Hereafter; the balance in understanding the divine values and aspects of humanity; positive in realising a good relationship between God, humans, the universe and the Hereafter; recognising the reality of God and the divine nature behind the reality of existence; monotheism is a source of belief about the existence of Allāh that is understood from His Revelations to the Messenger of Allāh; and based on the *Tawhîdic* paradigm. That is the unicity or oneness of God that everything in Islām is built upon it. No act of worship or rituals, inwardly or outwardly, has any meaning or value if this concept is in any way compromised. This *Tawhîdic* paradigm is related to the unification process 'aiming to unify diverse existents, such as physical objects, religions, cultures and fields of inquiry, was motivated by the belief in the oneness of knowledge' (Ajami, 2016).

In addition to the *Tawhîdic* dimension, there is also an ethical (moral – *akhlāq*) dimension of Islāmic worldview. This is reflected in the following verse. Allāh says:

لَّيْسَ ٱلْبِرَّ أَن تُوَلُّواْ وُجُوهَكُمْ قِبَلَ ٱلْمَشْرِقِ وَٱلْمَغْرِبِ وَلَٰكِنَّ ٱلْبِرَّ مَنْ ءَامَنَ بِٱللَّهِ وَٱلْيَوْمِ ٱلْءَاخِرِ وَٱلْمَلَٰٓئِكَةِ وَٱلْكِتَٰبِ وَٱلنَّبِيِّۦنَ وَءَاتَى ٱلْمَالَ عَلَىٰ حُبِّهِۦ ذَوِى ٱلْقُرْبَىٰ وَٱلْيَتَٰمَىٰ وَٱلْمَسَٰكِينَ وَٱبْنَ ٱلسَّبِيلِ وَٱلسَّآئِلِينَ وَفِى ٱلرِّقَابِ وَأَقَامَ ٱلصَّلَوٰةَ وَءَاتَى ٱلزَّكَوٰةَ وَٱلْمُوفُونَ بِعَهْدِهِمْ إِذَا عَٰهَدُواْ ۖ وَٱلصَّٰبِرِينَ فِى ٱلْبَأْسَآءِ وَٱلضَّرَّآءِ وَحِينَ ٱلْبَأْسِ ۗ أُوْلَٰٓئِكَ ٱلَّذِينَ صَدَقُواْ ۖ وَأُوْلَٰٓئِكَ هُمُ ٱلْمُتَّقُونَ

- *Righteousness is not in turning your faces towards the east or the west. Rather, the righteous are those who believe in Allāh, the Last Day, the angels, the Books, and the prophets; who give charity out of their cherished wealth to relatives, orphans, the poor, 'needy' travellers, beggars, and for freeing captives; who establish prayer, pay alms-tax, and keep the pledges they make; and who are patient in times of suffering, adversity, and in 'the heat of' battle. It is they who are true 'in faith', and it is they who are mindful 'of Allāh'.*

(Al-Baqarah 2:177, interpretation of the meaning)

These fundamental elements of ethical and moral values act as integrating principles as they render the standards of behaviours and values into a coherent order as a unified system forming the Islāmic worldview. This is how Muslims view the realities of the world and interact with the world through the lens of an Islāmic worldview (Rassool, 2023). Based on the characteristics, the Islāmic or Qur'ānic worldview is basically an ethical and monotheistic worldview that stems from the *Tawhîdic* paradigm.

It is worth noting of the perception Abdul Hamid Abu Sulayman (2011) on the characteristics of the worldview among Muslims. He argues that:

[a] genuinely Islāmic worldview is down-to-earth, comprehensive, law-governed, positive, and disciplined. Unfortunately, however, the predominant worldview among Muslims, which purports falsely to be 'Islamic,' is theoretical, atomistic, passive, and selective – its purpose being to justify or conceal a quasi-sacerdotal distortion of knowledge and the facts and the inability to master a comprehensive, objective scientific approach to research and analysis.

(p. 3)

Abu Sulayman is suggesting that an authentic Islāmic worldview is practical, all-encompassing, rule-based, and constructive. Regrettably, the prevailing worldview often misconstrued as 'Islamic' is theoretical, fragmented, inactive, and biased, primarily serving to mask a distorted understanding of knowledge and hinder the adoption of an inclusive and unbiased scientific approach to research and analysis. This blemished worldview seemed to be still prevalent in Muslim-majority countries, especially among the acculturated and Western-oriented Muslims. At this stage, it would be valuable to examine Ibn Al-Haytham's philosophy on scientific research noting that Islāmic research philosophy is anchored in Islāmic worldview, epistemology and Islāmic ontology.

Ibn Al-Haytham's philosophy on scientific research

Ibn Al-Haytham (Abū ʿAli Al-Ḥasan ibn al-Ḥasan ibn) has been identified as the main pioneer who's responsible for exploring the scientific methodology

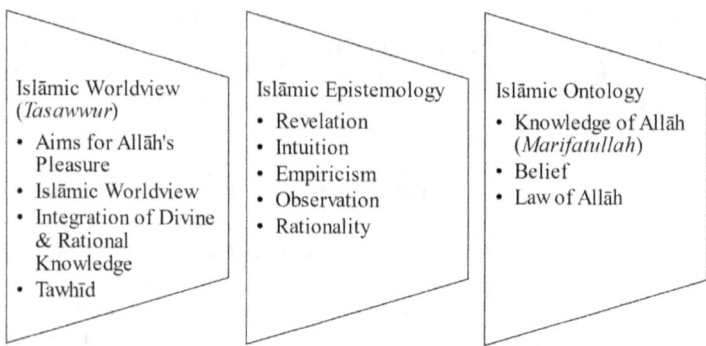

Figure 2.3 Ibn Al-Haytham's philosophy on scientific research.
Source: Adapted from Alias and Hanapi (2015).

and is often referred to as the 'world's first true scientist' (Al-Khalili, 2009). In his scientific inquiries, which concentrated on studying optics and vision, he relied on experimentation and controlled testing (Al-Haytham & Al-Hasan, 1983). Ibn Al-Haytham believed in knowledge integration or the unicity of knowledge unifying mathematical, physical and physiological aspects into a single coherent scientific approach. Ibn Al-Haytham's philosophy on scientific research is based on Islāmic *tasawwur*, Islāmic epistemology and Islāmic ontology. Figure 2.3 presents Ibn Al-Haytham's philosophy on scientific research.

One of the components of Ibn Al-Haytham's philosophy on scientific research is *tasawwur*, which may be construed as a worldview. In the literal sense, the concept of *tasawwur* means perception, presumption, mental attitude or a viewpoint on matters (Al-Qasimiy, 1989, p. 755; Ibn Manzur, 1994, p. 473). This concept has also been described as imagination, contemplation, reflection and conception. Islāmic scholars have used different terminology to portray the meaning of Islāmic *tasawwur* (Alias & Hanapi, 2015). For Ibn Al-Haytham, the scope of Islāmic *tasawwur* includes the embodiment of both the material and metaphysical/spiritual realms in his compliance with Islāmic beliefs and practices. The Islāmic *tasawwur* is also related to *Tawhīd* (the Unicity or oneness of God). His closeness to Islāmic practices enables him to undertake scientific research because 'the research could become a tool to always allow him to be close to Allāh' (Alias & Hanapi, 2015, p. 86). This is reflected in his statements:

> I am truly committed to give my views, since this could take me closer to Allāh, allow the factor that permits this to be blessed by Him and the signs that make me obey Him and be conscious of Him.
>
> (Ibn Abi Usaybi'ah, 1965, p. 552)

The pulling factor for Ibn Al-Haytham to seek in this pursuit of excellence in his scientific research is through the blessing of Allāh (*Mardhatillah*), the Almighty. Ibn Al-Haytham's intention in the pursuit of scientific research is reflected in the follow verse:

وَمِنَ ٱلنَّاسِ مَن يَشْرِى نَفْسَهُ ٱبْتِغَآءَ مَرْضَاتِ ٱللَّهِ ۗ وَٱللَّهُ رَءُوفٌ بِٱلْعِبَادِ

- *And of the people is he who sells himself, seeking means to the approval of Allāh, and Allāh is kind to [His] servants.*

(Al-Baqarah, 2:207, interpretation of meaning)

Ibn Al-Haytham (1989) suggested that "the faculty of judgment concerning things that have been seen by human is actually has been established in the soul (*al-nafs*). Hence, the ability to evaluate does not need much effort or deliberation because it happens naturally" (Ibn Al-Haytham, cited in Alias & Hanapi, 2015, p. 86). He claimed that his experimental research 'might [not] be the absolute truth but rather the absolute truth comes from Allāh, the Almighty' (Othman, 2009, p. 141). That is the absolute truth is from divine knowledge and known only to God, despite the failings of human nature to believe that our own perceptions are reality.

Al-Haytham's scientific methodology is also based on an Islāmic epistemology based on holistic knowledge, which is an integration of transmitted knowledge (*Al-ulum al-naqliyah*) and rational knowledge (*Al-ulum al-aqliyah*), thus providing a dynamic and interactive process. It has been suggested that:

> [t]he process of bringing the religious and the secular elements together is, from the Islāmic point of view, a restoration of the link between reason and revelation, or between the role of the mind in appreciating (comprehending and interpreting) revelation and guiding the mind by means of the revelation's objectives, its comprehensive and universal outlook, and its living and civilization values. Thus, the joining of the two wings in the pursuit of reform in an intellectual process in its methodology and style.
>
> (AbuSulayman, 1993, p. 21)

What AbuSulayman is suggesting is that uniting religious and secular aspects within Islām involves reconnecting reason and revelation, allowing the intellect to grasp and interpret divine guidance while also using revelation to direct the intellect towards comprehensive objectives, universal perspectives, and societal values. This integration for the purpose of reform represents an intellectual approach that harmonizes both elements, guiding the methodology and manner of this process. The two main sources of knowledge can be subdivided into divine revelation (*wahy*), inspiration (*ilham*), intuition, intellect (*'aql*) and senses

(Langgulung, 1986, pp. 19–23; Ahmad, 2010, pp. 117–119). In his scientific endeavour, Ibn Al-Haytham used independent reasoning (*ijtihad*) supplemented by intuition or inspiration and observation via sensory faculties. He stated that '[i]n my opinion, truth cannot be achieved unless there is an understanding that its elements are based on sensory perception and its form is based on mental reasoning' (cited in Ibn Abi Usaybi'ah, 1965, p. 552). But above all, Ibn Al-Haytham developed his own methodology of observation, development of hypothesis, experimentation and proving or refuting (reasoning) the basic hypothesis or premise.

Islāmic ontology literally refers to theory about the existence from an Islāmic perspective. This means it is the study of Islāmic philosophy related to the existence of God, creation, human, environment and of what constitutes reality. It has been propounded that discourse on ontology focuses on 'the scope of the knowledge; whether it is limited to the physical ('*alam al-syahadah*) or transverses the metaphysical realm ('*alam al-ghayb*)' (Abdullah, 2010, p. 19). The reality of existence is based on the universal laws of God (*Al-Sunan Rabaniyyah*). These universal laws of Allāh are not just restricted to matters pertaining to nature but to societies and human interaction. This enables the undertaking of observation and rationality using the law of cause and effect. This is reflected in the statement made by Al-Haytham (1989) that:

[t]he characterisation of the eye by this property is one of the things that show the wisdom of the Artificer, great be His glory, the skilfulness of His work and the successful and skilful manner in which nature has arranged the instruments of sight . . ."

(p. 103)

Ibn Al-Haytham's philosophy of scientific research was heavily influenced by the manifestations of God's greatness and the universal laws of Allāh.

In contrast to modern Western philosophy, Islāmic ontology accepts the existence of the Hereafter, and Islāmic epistemology accepts knowledge acquired through divine revelation. There are several takeaways that can be deduced from Al-Haytham's philosophy on scientific research. One of the prime objectives of the Islāmic researcher is to make the Qurān and *Sunnah* the fundamental basis of scientific research based on the *Tawhîdic* paradigm. Divine revelation becomes the basic guide in scientific research supplemented with institution, observation, experiment and rationality based within the context of spiritual dimension. Both the combinations of the realm of physical and metaphysical should form a holistic approach to research methodology. The trilogy of Islāmic *tasawwur*, Islāmic epistemology and Islāmic ontology should be the platform to build research investigations. Above all, to follow in the footsteps of Ibn Al-Haytham is to achieve Allah's blessings.

References

Abdullah, A. R. (2010). *Philosophical Discourse of Historical Science and Thought*. Wacana falsafah sains sejarah dan pemikiran. Pulau Pinang: Pusat Kajian Pengurusan Pembangunan Islam (ISDEV), USM.

Abi-Hashem, N. (2017). Worldview, the concept of. In D. Leeming (Eds.), *Encyclopedia of Psychology and Religion*. Berlin & Heidelberg: Springer. https://doi.org/10.1007/978-3-642-27771-9_9357-6.

AbuSulayman, A. H. (1993). *Crisis in the Muslim Mind*. Herndon, VA: International Institute of Islāmic Thought.

AbuSulayman, A. H. (2011). *The Qur'ānic Worldview: A Springboard for Cultural Reform*. Herndon, VA: International Institute of Islāmic Thought (IIIT).

Ahmad, F. A. (2010). *Kaedah Pengurusan Institusi- institusi Pembangunan Berteraskan Islamdi Malaysia*. Selangor: UPENA.

Ajami, H. (2016). Oneness of knowledge in Islamic philosophy. *Open Access Library Journal*, 3, 1–4.

Akhmetova, E., & Rafikov, I. (2021). *Course on Methodology of Scientific Research and Concept Formation (ITKI 6001)*. Georgia: Institute of Integrated Knowledge. Retrieved from http://ikiacademy.org.

Al-Haytham, al-Hasan Ibn Al-Hasan. (1983). *Kitab Al-Manazir* (Arabic ed.). Kuwait City: Al Majlis Al Watani lil Thaqafah wa al-Funun wa al-Adaab.

Al-Haytham, al-Hasan Ibn Al-Hasan. (1989). *The Optics of Ibn al-Haytham*, Book I–III: On Direct Vision, trans. Abdelhamid I. Sabra. London: Warburg Institute, University of London.

Alias, M. S., & Hanapi, M. S. (2015). Ibn Al-Haytham's philosophy on scientific research applied in Islamic research methodology: Analysis from *tasawwur*, epistemology and ontology perspectives. *International Journal of Business, Humanities and Technology*, 5(1), 83.

Al-Khalili, J. (2009). *The 'First True Scientist'*. Retrieved November 14, 2022, from http://news.bbc.co.uk/2/hi/science/nature/7810846.stm

Al-Qasimiy, Ahmad Mokhtar bin 'Umar Muhyi al-Din Sobir bin 'Ali. (1989). *Al-Mu'jam al-'Arabi al-Asasi*. Tunisia: Larousse.

Bucaille, M. (2000). *The Bible, The Qur'an and Science the Holy Scriptures Examined in the Light of Modern Knowledge*. CreateSpace Independent Publishing Platform.

Cohen, L., Manion, L., & Morrison, K. R. B. (2017). *Research Methods in Education*. London: Routledge.

Creswell, J. W., & Plano Clark, V. L. (2007). *Designing and Conducting Mixed Method Research*. London: Sage Publications.

Dar al-Ifta Al-Missriyyah. (2022). *The Research Methodology in Traditional Islāmic Scholarship*. Retrieved from www.dar-alifta.org/foreign/ViewArticle.aspx?ID=113.

Foundation for Science, Technology and Civilisation. (2006) *Islāmic Science, the Scholar and Ethics*. UK. Retrieved from https://muslimheritage.com/islamic-science-scholar-ethics/.

Guba, E., & Lincoln, Y. (1994). Competing paradigms in qualitative research. In N. Denzin & Y. Lincoln (Eds.), *Handbook on Qualitative Research* (pp. 105–118). Thousand Oaks, CA: Sage Publications.

Hassan, M. (n.d.). *What Is Philosophy – Definition, Methods, Types*. Retrieved from https://researchmethod.net/what-is-philosophy/.

Heron, J., & Reason, P. (1997). A participatory inquiry paradigm. *Qualitative Inquiry*, 3(3), 274–294.

Ibn Abi Usaybi'ah, Ahmad Ibn Qasim. (1965). *Uyun al-Anba' fi Tabaqat al-Atibba*. Beirut, Lubnan: Dar Maktabah al-Hayah.

Ibn Manzur, Abi al-Fadl Jamal al-Din Muhammad bin Mukram al-Afriqiy al-Misriy. (1994). *Lisan al-'Arab* (Vol. 5). Beirut, Lubnan: Dar Sadir.

Ibrahim, F. A., & Kahn, H. (1987). Assessment of world views. *Psychological Reports*, 60(1), 163–176. https://doi.org/10.2466/pr0.1987.60.1.163.

Langgulung, H. (1986). *Introduction of Islamic Civilization in Education*. Kuala Lumpur: Dewan Bahasa danPustaka.

Malkawi, F. H. (2014). *Epistemological Integration: Essentials of an Islāmic Methodology*. Herndon, VA: The International Institute of Islāmic Thought.

Omer, S. (2016). *Islam and Tradition*. Retrieved November 11, 2022, from www.islamicity.org/9068/islam-and-tradition/.

Othman, M. Y. (2009). *Science, Society and Religion (Sains, Masyarakatdan Agama)*. Kuala Lumpur: Utusan Publications & Distributors Sdn. Bhd.

Rassool, G. H. (2023). *Islāmic Psychology: The Basics*. Oxford: Routledge.

Saunders, M., Lewis, P., & Thornhill, A. (2015). *Research Methods for Business Students* (7th ed.). London: Pearson,

Taqiyuddin, M. (2020). In search of Islāmic definition of worldview: Elements, and its characters. *Zawiyah: Jurnal Pemikiran Islam*, 6(2), 206–222.

Utz, A. (2011). *Psychology From an Islāmic Perspective*. Riyadh: International Islāmic Publishing House.

3 Principles of Islāmic ethics

Issues in conducting research

Introduction

The concept of ethics is literally translated in Arabic terminology as *akhlāq* (singular, *khuluq*). Ethics is a concept with reference to knowledge of moral or moral principles, and from an Islāmic perspective the principle of morality (or *akhlaq*), virtues, duties and attitudes. Ethics is context-based and is related to beliefs, culture and traditions as these have an influence on worldview. Islāmic ethics has been referred to as "a code of conduct that calls for humankind to undertake a continuous process of self-purification, in thought, feelings and emotions (*Tazkiyah an nafs*); in social interactions through intentions and deeds that benefit other human beings as well as other creations of God; in using the resources that God has given him in a wise manner; and in bringing him closer to the ideal as described by the Prophet: 'the best amongst you are those who are the owners of the best morality'" (Sattar, 2017). In relation to Islāmic medical ethics, this is referred as 'the methodology of analysing and resolving the ethical issues that arise in healthcare practice or research based on the Islāmic moral and legislative sources (primarily the Qur'ān and Sunnah) and aims at achieving the goals of Islāmic morality' (Woodman et al., 2019, p. 1).

Ethical or moral values are embedded in Islāmic theology in the personal and professional life of Muslims. In Islām, there is no separation between ethical values and religious constructs. Islāmic scholars argue that ethical deliberation is inseparable from the religion itself, which emphasises the integration of body, mind, soul, metaphysical and spiritual realms and between ethics and jurisprudence (Al-Faruqi, 1982; Daar & Al Khitamy, 2001). Islāmic ethics are universal in its orientation and transcends the limitations of time, place and tradition. Islāmic ethics, an extension of Islāmic law (*Shari'ah*), differ from its Western counterpart as it's broader in perspectives and are based on the Qur'ān and the *Sunnah*. The use rationality or analogical reasoning (*Ijtihad* or *Qiyas*) is used when the issues concerned are beyond the scope of the Qur'ān and the *Sunnah*. The source of influence in the development of philosophy of ethics and bioethics was as a

DOI: 10.4324/9781003346241-3

result of the Islāmic Renaissance period between the ninth and seventeenth centuries and beyond. Islām civilisation experienced significant scientific, cultural and economic developments. Muslim classical, scholars including, Abu Ali Ahmad b. Muhammad bin Ya'kub Ibn Miskawayh known as Ibn Miskawayh. He was the author of the first major Islāmic work on philosophical ethics titled the 'Refinement of Character' (*Tahdhīb al-Akhlāq*) focusing on practical ethics, conduct and refinement of character (Rassool & Luqman, 2022, p. 48). Mohammed Zakariya Al-Rāzī wrote about medical ethics in his book 'The Comprehensive Book of Medicine' (*Kitab al Hawi fi al-tibb*). Al-Rāzī in the

> Epistle to One of his Pupils, he suggested that a noble physician is a man who lives in self-restraint, especially when he treats women, and who keeps the secrets of his patients. He insists that the art of the physician extends to the rich and to the poor
>
> (Koetschet, 2018)

This chapter focuses on the examination of Western and Islāmic ethics; provides an overview of ethics and bioethics guidelines in the Islāmic world and Islāmic ethical guidelines for research.

Ethics: an international perspective

The paradigm of Western-oriented bioethics are based on 'the four principles': respect for autonomy, beneficence, non-maleficence and justice (Beauchamp & Childress, 2013). In effect, ethical decision-making is based on the four principles. However, these principles are derived from Judeo–Christian traditions and form the basis of international ethical guidelines and various codes of ethics. There are several universal documentations of the foundational principles of research ethics from a Western-oriented paradigm. The Council for International Organizations of Medical Sciences (CIOMS, 2016) has published the International ethical guidelines for health-related research involving humans. Other documents include the Nuremberg Code (1947), which focuses on the basic principles of research in order to satisfy moral, ethical and legal concepts; The Declaration of Helsinki Human Experimentation: Code of Ethics (World Medical Association, 2013); The Belmont Report. Ethical principles and guidelines for the protection of human subjects of research (Department of Health, Education, and Welfare et al., 2014).

In relation to psychological research in the United Kingdom (UK), the British Psychological Society (2014) published the Code of Human Research Ethics that sets out a set of general principles that are applicable to all research contexts and to cover all research with human participants. These guidelines can be used by funding bodies and academic institutions to inform

Principles of Islāmic ethics 37

their own research ethics. The principles of ethics adopted in these guidelines include:

- 'Respect for the autonomy, privacy and dignity of individuals and communities.
- Scientific integrity.
- Social responsibility.
- Maximising benefit and minimising harm.'

(BPS, 2014, p. 7)

The British Association for Counselling and Psychotherapy has produced ethical guidelines for researching counselling and psychotherapy (Bond, 2004). The aim of the guidelines is 'to promote and inform good research practice. The guidelines are applicable to the wide range of research positions and methodologies that contribute to the advancement of knowledge and understanding in the field of counselling and psychotherapy' (Bond, 2004, p. 4). The ethical dimensions include trustworthiness, managing the risks, relationships with research participants (consent, protection of personally sensitive information, researching areas of vulnerability in people's lives and cultural and social diversity), research integrity and research governance. The American Psychology Association's (APA, 2017) ethical principles of psychologists and code of conduct are based on the principle of beneficence and non-maleficence, fidelity and responsibility, integrity, justice and respect for people's rights and dignity.

In the psychological research context, the universal principles of ethics including autonomy, beneficence, non-maleficence and justice may have a valid application. However, this perspective is not universally agreed upon. Christakis (1992) argues that culture shapes both the content and forms of moral and ethical systems, and ethical behaviour needs to fit within the framework of the local context. That is, ethics are culturally bound. In this case, one would question to whether Western research ethical principles are reflected in Islāmic research ethics. However, the perspective of respect for persons, beneficence, non-malfeasance, fidelity, respect for autonomy, self-interest and justice is universally agreed upon (Beauchamp & Childress, 2013).

Pillars of research ethics in Islāmic psychology

The root of moral or ethical behaviours from an Islāmic perspective is based on three main sources: Belief in the unity of God and innate nature(*Al-fitrah*),faculty of reasoning (*al-'aql*) and divine revelation (*Al-wahy*) (Al-Bar & Chamsi-Pasha, 2015, p. 1). Though this is based in the context of Islāmic medical ethics, it is also universally applicable to Islāmic psychology research ethics.

38 *Principles of Islāmic ethics*

The *fitrah* is an important concept in Islāmic psychology because it is embedded in the human soul and an essential facet of human behaviour. It has been suggested that

> [t]he Qur'ān makes it clear that we all born with the innate sense of the truth and belief of God's existence and we possess a certain intuitive knowledge of the moral good. The essence of the *fitrah* is the natural spiritual nature of man and having a predisposition to submit to the One God. The *fitrah* embodies the notion that humans begin life not with blank moral slates (tabula rasa) but are hardwired with an innate sense of morality and truth.
>
> (Rassool, 2023, p. 98)

There is evidence to suggest that humans have an innate circuit with a sense of moral virtues and judgement. Babies, even before they can speak or walk, have been found to feel empathy and compassion; judging the good and bad; act to soothe those in distress; and have a rudimentary sense of justice (Bloom, 2013). This *fitrah* is our natural moral compass to guide us towards the truth and is applicable to nature of all humankind in diverse tribes and nations.

The second pillar is *'aql* (Reason, intellect): *'Aql* in Islāmic psychology is the rational faculty of the soul or mind. It has also been translated as 'dialectical reasoning' (Esposito, 2004, p. 22). Al-Jawzi (2004) suggested that the concept is restricted to only four meanings: (1) sensory-cognitive processing of information; (2) to designate self-evident things or truths; (3) that which is gained through experience; and (4) restraining oneself from the heart's vain desires [ethical intelligence]. The *'aql* is regarded as one of the gifts bestowed to humans by God, the Almighty. We use our intellect to maintain our moral good, and it is essential in the development of ethical intelligence. This enables humankind to make critical judgement on what is right or wrong (*Halal* or *haram*) and develop creative thinking. There are a number of verses in the Qur'ān that focus on those with an absence of intellect or the power of reasoning or those who fail to use the intellect for guidance. However, Allāh rebukes those who fail to use the intellect. Allāh says in the Qur'ān

إِنَّ شَرَّ ٱلدَّوَابِّ عِندَ ٱللَّهِ ٱلصُّمُّ ٱلْبُكْمُ ٱلَّذِينَ لَا يَعْقِلُونَ

- *Indeed, the worst of living creatures in the sight of Allāh are the deaf, dumb who do not use reason.*

    (Al-Anfal 8:22, interpretation of the meaning).

The final pillar is *wahy* (divine revelation). That is the process of divine revelation of Allāh commands to His Prophets and Messengers as well as the

Principles of Islāmic ethics 39

revelation itself. In relation to the Prophet and Messenger of Allāh (ﷺ), this is reflected in the following verse of the Qur'ān:

$$\text{وَمَا يَنطِقُ عَنِ ٱلْهَوَىٰ}$$
$$\text{إِنْ هُوَ إِلَّا وَحْيٌ يُوحَىٰ}$$

- Nor does he speak of (his own) desire.
- It is only a Revelation revealed

(Al-Najm 53:3–4, interpretation of the meaning).

According to the exegesis of Ibn Kathir (2000), Prophet Muhammad (ﷺ) was sent

as a Mercy for all that exists; He does not speak of His Desire. (Nor does he speak of desire), means, asserting that nothing the Prophet utters is of his own desire or wish. (It is only a revelation revealed.), means, he only conveys to the people what he was commanded to convey, in its entirety without additions or deletions.

This is the proposition that '*Wahy* guides the first two pillars [*al-fitrah* and '*aql*] and protects everyone from corruption. *Wahy* also focuses on the possibility of how to restore the masses to the way they existed before, in their prime unaltered form' (Al-Bar & Chamsi-Pasha, 2015, p. 2).

Kasule (2004) has suggested that there is a need to examine the following categories to ensure that the research is within the Islāmic ethic paradigm: Intention of research, certainty and doubts, risks or injuries, hardship and custom or precedent. Table 3.1 presents the Islāmic ethic criteria for research.

Ethical considerations must be given to the different stages of research, from design to development. Kasule (2004) argues that if the purpose of the research is ill-conceived, doubtful or uncertain, accompanied with high risks then that research is morally prohibited. Islāmic research ethics framework is based on (1) public interest/common good (*maslaha*) and (2) no harm, no harassment (Sachedina, 2007, 2009). Other principles and considerations include:

- The virtuous researcher.
- Principle of 'enjoining good and forbidding wrong' (*al-amr bi'l-ma'ruf wa'n-nahy ani l-munkar*).
- Advocate for better standards of conduct in research.
- Reducing suffering and unnecessary experiments on animals (Rattani & Hyder, 2019, p. 84).
- Ecological validity of research.

Table 3.1 Islāmic ethical criteria for research

Criteria	Explanations
Intention of research	If the purpose of the proposed research is ill intentioned, ill-conceived or the method used in determining the objective is scientifically invalid, then the research project is not ethically acceptable.
Certainty and doubts	There must be some empirical evidence of low efficacy of the current standard of care and treatment or potential benefits of the proposed new treatment before an experiment is authorised.
Risks or injuries	Balance between harms and risks. For example, these risks have to be balanced against the harm caused by the disease and the potential benefit of the proposed new treatment (risk/benefit ratio).
Hardship	Necessity legalises the prohibited. An example of such a situation is participation in a phase I trial. The case of Covid-19 pandemic with no available vaccine, then it would be permissible to expose healthy volunteers to the potential harm of participation in such trials for the benefit of the community.
Custom or precedent	The principle of custom (or standard of care) is used to define the standards of good clinical practice.

Source: Adapted from Kasule (2004).

Research ethics: an Islāmic perspective

In recent decades, many Muslim-majority countries are making attempts to develop clinical research guidelines. This development is due to the emergence of many new universities and research centres. However, it is reported that countries in the Middle East operate under considerably fewer strict research ethical guidelines than their Western world (Kermani, 2010). With the expansion of clinical research in the Middle East, ethical issues involving the use of human subjects are being formulated, especially in the biomedical field. Alahmad et al. (2012) provide a review of national research ethics regulations and guidelines in Middle East Arab countries. The findings showed that there were different levels and kinds of research ethics regulations and guidelines and the majority of the documents refer to one or more international documents on biomedical research ethics. Obtaining informed consent is at the top of the listed protections, followed by obligation of scientific validity and review by an ethics committee, benefits, risks ratios and confidentiality. The authors conclude that, compared with international documents, most of the research ethics documents in use are limited in their structure, contents and reference to international guidelines.

Principles of Islāmic ethics 41

Islāmic ethical guidelines of research are derived from the purposes and principles of the Higher Objectives of Islāmic law (*Maqasid al-Shari'ah*):

- protection of religion (*Deen*);
- maintenance of life (*Nafs*);
- protection of intellect (*'Aql*);
- preservation of honour and progeny (*Nasl*); and
- protection of wealth (*Mal*).

Research in psychology or biomedical ethics should be conducted for one of the five reasons. In effect, anything that preserves one of these five purposes is regarded as beneficial. Beside these purposes (*Maqasid*), there is also the Islāmic legal maxims (*Qawā'id Fiqhiyyah*) Kasule (2005) suggests that the five principles of the Higher Objectives of Islāmic law (*Maqasid al-Shari'ah*) resolve conflicts between and among the *Maqasid*. The application of the Islāmic legal maxims, based on five categories have particular significance to Islāmic research ethics. The five normative Islāmic legal maxims are presented in Table 3.2.

Table 3.2 Five normative legal maxims of Islāmic law

Maxim	Principle	Explanations
Intention	*Al-umuru bi-maqasidiha:* Acts are judged by the intention behind them.	Research is judged by its underlying and not expressed intentions. What is the purpose of the research?
Harm	*Ad-dararu yuzal:* Harm must be eliminated.	Research is allowed if benefit expected from the experimental therapy outweighs the potential risks. Removing potential risks of harm and hazards. Risk/benefit ratio.
Certainty v/s Doubt	*Al-yaqinu la yazulu bish-shakk:* Certainty is not overruled by doubt.	Research on new treatment modalities is permitted if there are doubts about existing modalities.
Hardship v/s Facility	*Al-mashaqqatu tujlab at-taysir:* Hardship begets facility.	Research in achieving ease and not hardship. Concept of justice. Evidence-based overruling intuition and opinions.
Custom	*Al-'addatu muhakkamatun:* Cultural usage shall have the weight of law.	Define standards of good clinical practice. Custom is the basis of judgement.

Source: Adapted from Kasule (2005).

The maxims of Islāmic law (*Qawa'id al-Fiqhiyyah*) that 'Harm must be removed' (*lā ḍarar wa lā ḍirār*) and hardship begets facility (*al-mashaqqatu tajlib al-taysīr*) are relevant and appropriate in the research context. Muhsin et al. (2021) suggested that

> The difference between harm maxim and hardship (*mashaqqah*) maxim is that the former is applied when its elimination or prevention is feasible while the latter is used by begetting facility to remove obstacles and to ease the burden of lives. The application of hardship maxim is restricted by another maxim 'whatever is permissible owing to some excuse ceases to be permissible with the disappearance of that excuse.' It means that facilitation is valid only in the presence of impediment, and once it is removed, the original ruling is restored to full effect.

When examining the intention of the research, it is important to reflect on the following *Hadīth* the Prophet (ﷺ). This is one of the greatest and most comprehensive *Hadīth* as it sets one of the most important principles in the religion of Islām, specifically as it touches upon almost every deed in Islām. It is narrated on the authority of Umar Ibn Al-Khatam who said: I heard the Messenger of Allah (ﷺ) say:

> Surely, All actions are but driven by intentions and, verily, every man shall have but which he intended. Thus, he whose migration was for Allah and His Messenger, (then) his migration was for Allah and His Messenger; and he whose migration was to achieve some worldly benefit or to take a woman in marriage, his migration was for that which he migrated.
>
> (Bukhari and Muslim)

From an Islāmic perspective, the purpose of research is explicitly intended to promote welfare and enjoined what is good and forbid what is wrong. Auda (2021) suggested that '[r]esearch, disciplines and systems that do not centralise faith and noble human aims must be challenged' (p. 34). There is also the subprinciples related to intention. Mustafa (2012) provides an example that the 'means do not justify the ends (*Al waṣā'il lahā ḥukm al Maqāsid*) and, therefore, immoral methods used to achieve beneficial [psychological] purposes are deemed impermissible' (p. 2). Thus, research project is not ethically acceptable. The principle of certainty (*yaqīn*): This maxim in essence that certainty is not overruled by doubt. If there is a doubt or limited evidence on the efficacy of psychological interventions or research methodologies, then the activity becomes redundant. The prevention or removal of harm (*darar*) needs to be considered in human experimentation.

On the authority of Abu Sa'eed al-Khudree (may Allah be pleased with him), that the Messenger of Allah said (ﷺ): There should be neither harming (*darar*) nor reciprocating harm (*dirar*) (Ibn Majah (a)). This unambiguous statement

Principles of Islāmic ethics 43

means that all forms of harm and of wrongly reciprocating harm are prohibited in Islām. The scholars have broken down 'harm' into two categories. The first category includes acts that only harm others. The second category includes acts that brings some benefit to the individual but may also cause harm to society in any shape or form. It has been suggested that 'the avoidance of harm has priority over the pursuit of a benefit of equal or lesser worth' (Mustafa, 2012, p. 2).

Inherent within this principle, it the sub-principle of responsibility and accountability that have been implemented since the early days of Islāmic civilisation. Scholars in Islāmic law explain that an individual must be proficient in the particular field he is a practitioner or a researcher. Research psychologists are required to be competent in conducting research, provide safeguards for the well-being of the participants the data should be accurate and transparent and the methodology must be appropriate (Afifi, 2007, Rattani & Hyder, 2019). Amr b. Shu'aib, on his father's authority, said his grandfather reported God's Messenger (ﷺ) as saying, 'Anyone who practices medicine when he is not known as a practitioner will be held responsible'* (ﷺ) (Abu Dawud and Nasa'i). This *Hadīth* may also be applicable to the responsibility and accountability of the research psychologists. The principles of beneficence and non-maleficence are relevant here. The aims beneficence and non-maleficence are to guide the research psychologists in making ethical decisions regarding the design and methodology of their research in the interest of their studied population. Beneficence is an ethical principle to promote moral good and action. In the context of research, the Muslim psychologists are obligated to, always and without exception, promote and maintain the interest of the research participants. This also apply in the case of administering psychological therapeutic interventions. Under the principle of beneficence, researchers must strive towards excellence, maximise benefits for the participants. Non-maleficence is related to the prevention of harms and exploitation of the research participants. Another principle relating to beneficence is striving to do well or excel in doing things well (*Ihsan*) in everything. *Ihsan* is one of the most important principles of Islām. It was narrated from Shaddad bin Aws that the Messenger of Allah (ﷺ) said: 'Allah has prescribed Al-Ihsan (proficiency) in all things' (Ibn Majah (b)).

The principle of justice is relevant in the ethical dimension of research. Its inclusion as a requirement in the ethical review of human research is relatively a new phenomenon. In the ethics of research involving human subjects, the principle of justice refers to having 'a fair distribution of burdens and benefits in the participant experience and the research outcomes' (Pieper & Thomson, 2013, p. 99). This relate to the question of who should receive the benefits of research and bear its burdens. The Belmont Report (1979) have identified accepted formulations of just ways to distribute burdens and benefits.

These formulations are (1) to each person an equal share, (2) to each person according to individual need, (3) to each person according to individual effort, (4) to each person according to societal contribution, and (5) to each person according to merit.

In its broader sense, justice in its general context is the fair selection of research participants and to design research so that its burdens and benefits are shared equitably. The principle of autonomy, in psychological research refers to the acknowledgement of, and respect for the population being studied. Two ethical convictions, in relation to autonomy,. have been identified in the Belmont Report. The first that individuals should be treated as autonomous agents and the second ethical conviction maintains that persons with diminished autonomy deserve extra protection (Lysaught, 2004). Vulnerable persons are protected in Islāmic jurisprudence. Every Muslim is bestowed with legal capacity except those who are minors, those in sleep and the insane. Legal capacity means that 'the ability of a person to oblige, be obliged and conduct one's affairs by oneself' (Al-Sabouni, 1978). One of the Islāmic legal maxims stated that: 'Whoever is deprived of legal capacity is exempted from a legal obligation' (Olayiwola, 2016). This is highlighted in a *Hadith* of the Prophet, when he said: Narrated Aisha, Ummul Mu'minin: The Messenger of Allah (ﷺ) said: There are three (persons) whose actions are not recorded: a sleeper till he awakes, an idiot till he is restored to reason, and a boy till he reaches puberty. Historically, Islāmic law protects people who fall within the category legal incapacity. A guardian is usually appointed in order to protect the individual. The principle of autonomy also obliges researchers to enable continuing informed consent, adhere to the proviso of confidentiality and privacy of their research participants, awareness of deception considerations, plagiarism considerations, and not withholding information about the research project.

Conclusion

The Islāmic research ethics theory on research is based on the five purposes of the Islāmic law, the *Maqasid al Shari'at* (religion, life, progeny, the mind and wealth). If any of these criteria is not met then the human subjects experimentation would be prohibited in Islāmic research. Kasule (2005) suggested, 'Therapeutic research fulfils the purpose of protecting health and life; Infertility research fulfils the purpose of protecting progeny; Psychiatric research fulfils the purpose of protecting the mind; and the search for cheaper treatments fulfils the purpose of protecting wealth' (p. 1). Islāmic and Western research ethical systems consider the actions and outcomes of ethical decision-making and share the principles of doing good (beneficence), avoiding harm (nonmalfeasance), respect for autonomy, and fairness and equity (justice). Muslim research psychologists must continue to uphold these moral principles at all stages of the research development and implementation, and in research publication.

References

Abu Dawud and Nasa'i. *Mishkat al-Masabih 3504*. In-book reference: Book 16, Hadīth 52.
Abu Dawud. *Sunan Abi Dawud 4398*. In-book reference: Book 40, Hadith 48. English translation: Book 39, Hadith 4384.
Afifi, R. Y. (2007a). Biomedical research ethics: An Islāmic view – part I. *International Journal of Surgery*, 5(5), 292–296.
Alahmad, G., Al-Jumah, M., & Dierickx, K. (2012). Review of national research ethics regulations and guidelines in Middle Eastern Arab countries. *BMC Medical Ethics*, 13, 34.
Al-Bar, M. A., & Chamsi-Pasha, H. (2015). *Contemporary Bioethics: Islāmic Perspective*. New York: Springer Publishing.
Al-Faruqi, I. R. (1982). *Tawhid: Its Implications for Thought and Life*. Kuala Lumpur: International Institute for Islāmic Thought.
Al-Jawzi, A. A. (2004). *Akhbar al-Azkiya'*. Beirut: Dar Ibn Hazm.
Al-Sabouni, A. Al-Rahman. (1978). In Mustafaa Al-Siba'ie and Abd Al-Rahman Al-Sabounī, *Al-Madkhal Li-Dirasat Al-Fiqh Al-Islami* 2 at, 24 (4th ed.). Al-Maktaba'ah Al-Jadiih.
American Psychology Association. (2017). *Ethical Principles of Psychologists and Code of Conduct*. Retrieved from www.apa.org/ethics/code.
Auda, J. (2021). *Re-envisioning Islāmic Scholarship: Maqasid Methodology as a New Approach*. Swansea: Claritas Books.
Beauchamp, T., & Childress, J. F. (2013). *Principles of Biomedical Ethics* (7th ed.). New York: Oxford University Press.
The Belmont Report. (1979). *Ethical Principles and Guidelines for the Protection of Human Subjects of Research. The National Commission for the Protection of Human Subjects of Biomedical and Behavioral Research*. Retrieved from www.hhs.gov/ohrp/regulations-and-policy/belmont-report/read-the-belmont-report/index.html#xjust.
Bloom, P. (2013). *Just Babies: The Origins of Good and Evil*. New York: Crown.
Bond, T. (2004). *Ethical Guidelines for Researching Counselling and Psychotherapy*. Rugby: British Association for Counselling and Psychotherapy.
British Psychological Society. (2014). *Code of Human Research Ethics*. London: BPS.
Bukhari and Muslim. *Riyad as-Salihin. The Book of Miscellany*. Arabic/English book reference: Book 1, Hadīth 75.
Christakis, N. (1992). Ethics are local: Engaging cross-cultural variations in the ethics for clinical research. *Social Science & Medicine*, 35(9), 1070–1091.
CIOMS. (2016). *International Ethical Guidelines for Health-related Research Involving Humans* (4th ed.). Geneva: Council for International Organizations of Medical Sciences (CIOMS).
Daar, A. S., & Al Khitamy, A. B. (2001). Bioethics for clinicians: 21. Islāmic bioethics. *Canadian Medical Association Journal*, 164, 60–63.
Department of Health, Education, and Welfare, & National Commission for the Protection of Human Subjects of Biomedical and Behavioral Research. (2014). The Belmont report. Ethical principles and guidelines for the protection of human subjects of research. *The Journal of the American College of Dentists*, 81(3), 4–13.
Esposito, J. (2004). *The Oxford Dictionary of Islam*. Oxford paperback reference. Oxford: Oxford University Press.

Ibn Kathir. (2000). *Tafsir Ibn Kathir* (J. Abualrub, N. Khitab, H. Khitab, A. Walker, M. Al-Jibali, & S. Ayoub, Trans.). Riyadh: Darussalam Publishers and Distributors.

Ibn Majah (a) and ad-Daraqutnee. *Hadīth 32, 40 Hadīth an-Nawawi*. Ibn Majah (b). *Sunan Ibn Majah 3170*. In-book reference: Book 27, Hadīth 9. English translation: Vol. 4, Book 27, Hadīth 3170. Grade: Sahih (Darussalam).

Kasule, O. H. (2004). *Ethics and Etiquette of Human Research*. Paper presented at the International Scientific Convention Jointly Organized by the Jordan Society for Islāmic Medical Studies, the Jordan Medical Association and the Federation of Islāmic Medical Association at Amman, Jordan 15–17 July 2004.

Kasule, O. H. (2005). Ethics and etiquette of human research. *The Arab Journal of Psychiatry*, 16(1), 1–15.

Kermani, F. (2010). How to run clinical trials in the Middle East. *SCRIP*, 1–8.

Koetschet, P. (2018). Al-Rāzī, the clinician, Chapter Fifteen. In P. Pormann (Ed.), *1001 Cures, Medicines & Healthcare from Muslim Civilisation* (pp. 146–153). Manchester: FSTC House.

Lysaught, M. T. (2004). Respect: Or how respect for persons became respect for autonomy. *Journal of Medicine and Philosophy*, 29(6), 665–680.

Muhsin, M. S., Amanullah, M., & Zakariyah, L. (2021). *Other Relevant Sub-Maxims in the Elimination of Harm – Part Five*. Islamonweb. Retrieved from https://en.islamonweb. net/other-relevant-sub-maxims-in-the-elimination-of-harm-part-five.

Mustafa, Y. J. (2012). Islam and the four principles of medical ethics. *Medical Ethics*, Published Online, 1–5. https://doi.org/10.1136/medethics-2012-101309.

Olayiwola, S. (2016). Defence mechanism in criminal liability under Islāmic law. *International Journal of Innovative Legal & Political Studies*, 4(4), 19–29.

Pieper, I., & Thomson, C. J. (2013). Justice in human research ethics. A conceptual and practical guide. *Monash Bioethics Review*, 31(1), 99–116.

Rassool, G. Hussein. (2023). *Islāmic Psychology: The Basics*. Oxford: Routledge.

Rassool, G.H. & Luqman, M.M. (2022). *Foundations of Islamic Psychology*. Oxford: Routledge.

Rattani, A., & Hyder, A. A. (2019). Developing an Islāmic research ethics framework. *Journal of Religion and Health*, 58(1), 74–86.

Sachedina, A. (2007). The search for Islāmic bioethics principles. In R. E. Ashcroft, A. Dawson, H. Draper, & J. R. McMillian (Eds.), *Principles of Health Care Ethic* (pp. 241–251). Chichester: Wiley.

Sachedina, A. (2009). *Islāmic Biomedical Ethics: Principles and Application*. New York: Oxford University Press.

Sattar, N. (2017). *Ethics in Islam, the West and Muslim World*. Islāmic City. Retrieved from www.Islāmicity.org/12983/ethics-in-islam-the-west-and-muslim-world/.

Woodman, A., Al-Bar, M. A., & Chamsi-Pasha, H. (2019). Introduction to Islāmic medical ethic. *Journal of the British Islāmic Medical Association (JBIMA)*, 2(1), 1–5.

World Medical Association. (2013). *Amended Declaration of Helsinki – Ethical Principles for Medical Research Involving Human Subjects*. Retrieved from www.wma. net/policies-post/wma-declaration-of-helsinki-ethical-principles-for-medical-research-involving-human-subjects/.

4 Decolonisation, epistemological bias and limitations in psychology

Introduction

The post-colonial research studies in psychology with Muslim communities should be re-examined in the light of the widespread adoption and acceptance of paradigms, terminologies and research models alien to the Islāmic worldview, political and socioeconomic considerations and ontological framework. Muslim psychologists and researchers have, consciously and unconsciously, fallen into the trap of blind following of their 'Masters' Voice,' coined as 'Muslim Psychologists in the Lizard's Hole,' by Badri (1979). This following Prophetic epitaph echoes that blind following. It was narrated from Abu Hurairah that the Messenger of Allah said (ﷺ):

> You will most certainly follow the ways of those who came before you, arm's length by arm's length, forearm's length by forearm's length, hand span by hand span, until even if they entered a hole of a mastigure (lizard) you will enter it too.

They said: 'O Messenger of Allah, (do you mean) the Jews and the Christians?' He said: 'Who else?' (Ibn Majah). Awaad (2021) suggested that Badri was concerned about the 'ethnocentric, indiscriminate exportation of secular Western psychology' to Muslim psychologists under the guise of the 'scientific superiority' of the West. This state of affairs was due to colonisation, now replaced, by globalisation, and have induced an institutionalised system which has reproduced 'certain dynamics of regressiveness and orientalisation, and the lack of meaningful growth and development in research with Muslim populations' (Shaikh, 2023, p. 74). Thus, research philosophy, paradigms and methodologies need to be deconstructed from its Eurocentric epistemological and ontological conceptions. This chapter focuses on an examination of the decolonisation and deconstruction of psychology research, the epistemological ontological and research biases and its control and the limitations of Islāmic scholarship in the discipline of Islāmic psychology.

Status of psychology research

There are inherent epistemological and ontological assumptions that inform the nature and process of the research methodology. It is important to recognise that orientalist research brings some set of epistemological assumptions into the research process. However, even though researchers are instinctively unconscious of them, these assumptions, nevertheless, influence how they understand and interpret their data (Klenke, 2008, p. 16). In addition, bias, in research, often determines method of analysis, ways of interpretation of data and findings from a particular worldview, and is potentially misleading. In this context, biased research, being economical with the truth, is deemed to be unethical and immoral. The epistemological ontological and research biases are implicit in Western-oriented research in the developed and developing world and need to be deconstructed to create an indigenous or 'Islāmise' alternative paradigm. There are also some specific limitations in contemporary Islāmic scholarship in knowledge production which have had a significant impact on the development of critical thinking, *Ijtihad* (reasoning) and practice across different school of thought. These limitations have been identified by Auda (2021) to include:

> imitation (*taqlid*) of historical opinions versus referring to Revelation as a primary source of knowledge; partialism (*tajzi*) versus the wholism expressed and demanded by Revelation; apologism (*tabrir*) versus introspection and caution commanded by Revelation; contradiction (*tanaqud*) versus the consistency found in and encouraged by the Revelation; and deconstructionism (*tafkik*) versus the important differentiation between Revelation and cultural products.
>
> (p. 44)

Colonisation and globalisation of psychology research

Colonisation and now globalisation has permeated dominant Eurocentric democratic, secular and sociopolitical narratives and values to be deemed superior above other forms of knowing and knowledge production. To understand the current status of research scholarship, it is important to recognise and understand the historical impact of colonisation on the methodologies and production of knowledge. Mignolo (2010) preferred the use of the term coloniality. The term refers to 'a whole system of thought, a mentality, and a power structure to be universally applicable and there is "no modernity without coloniality"' (p. 3). The three fundamentals of coloniality include the coloniality of knowledge, the coloniality of power a nd the coloniality of being (Ndlovu-Gatsheni, 2013a, 2013b). The imposition of a Eurocentric knowledge-based cultural supremacy on knowledge production and dissemination lends itself to the view that psychology is a global enterprise. This is reflected in the statements that

> Psychological globalisation embraces every country throughout the world and is crystalised as 'The Three Worlds of Psychology.' In this theory, the United States is considered the first world because to date it is the major producer of psychological knowledge that is exported to both the second world of psychology (e.g., England, Canada, and Australia) and the third world of psychology (i.e., developing countries such as Nigeria, Cuba). This theory presumes that each of the three worlds has an unequal capacity to produce and disseminate psychological knowledge that shapes the field of psychology.
>
> (Lawson et al., 2007, p. 8)

Grosfoguel (2013) echoes the reality of the situation by enquiring about

> [h]ow is it possible that the canon of thought in all the disciplines of the Social Sciences and Humanities in the Westernised university is based on the knowledge produced by a few men from five countries in Western Europe (Italy, France, England, Germany and the USA)?
>
> (p. 74)

Thus colonialism, with its ideological political, socioeconomic and educational supremacy and ramifications produced an intellectual genocide which can be regarded as a form of 'epistemicide,' that is, the extermination of knowledge and ways of knowing (Boaventura de Sousa Santos, 2010). That is the extermination of indigenous knowledge in favour of superior knowledge from the colonialists.

The sequelae of post-colonial and globalisation on psychology have produced Muslim psychologists following blindly secular psychology in research, educational and clinical practice. Dudgeon and Walker (2015) suggest, 'Psychology colonises both directly through the imposition of universalising, individualistic constructions of human behaviour and indirectly through the negation' (p. 276). As a consequence, Muslim psychologists have been acculturated in an orientalist worldview instead of an Islāmic worldview in their research scholarship and clinical practice. This is not dissimilar to the effects of globalisation on mental health (Kirmayer & Minas, 2000). What is certain, however, is that psychology and applied psychology can no longer be dissociated from the global political, socioeconomic context that frames the lives of the global communities.

Problems with research in psychology

Before examining the bias in psychology research, it would be valuable to have a critical review of the epistemological and methodological biases encountered in psychology research. Since its inception, psychology has been a field dominated by research from Western, Educated, Industrialised, Rich, and Democratic (WEIRD) countries. There is an assumption in psychological research that human behaviours including cognitive and affective processes are universal based on sampling from a single subpopulation. However, there is now growing body of evidence suggests that this is not the case. Research findings from the behavioural sciences have indicated 'significant variation among human populations in diverse domains, such as visual perception, fairness, cooperation, spatial reasoning, categorisation and inferential induction, moral reasoning, reasoning styles, self-concepts and related motivations, and the heritability of IQ' (Henrich et al., 2010, p. 61). This raises ethical questions about the practice of drawing universal claims about human behaviours and experiences based on research samples from WEIRD societies. Another appropriate criticism of psychological research is they focused too narrowly on Americans, who comprise less than 12 percent of the world's population (Machery, 2010). Arnett (2008), after reviewing articles published in six premier American Psychological Association's journals, has identified that the contributors, samples and editorial leadership of the journals are predominantly American.

The methodological problems with research in psychology are highlighted when researchers tried to replicate the studies. The issues of selective and convenient sampling, exclusion criteria, ambiguous experimental procedure after designing the study which has led to epistemological biases. One of the largest replication study to date casts doubt on many published positive results of psychology research (Open Science Collaboration, 2015). The study replicated 100 experimental and correlational studies published in three psychology journals. The findings offer a clear conclusion and suggest that a large portion of replications produced weaker evidence for the original findings despite using materials provided by the original authors, review in advance for methodological fidelity and high statistical power to detect the original effect sizes. One interesting finding of the study showed that although 97 percent of original studies had statistically significant results, the replication studies showed that only 36 percent of replications had statistically significant results. However, the reproducibility project points to widespread publication of work that does not stand up to scrutiny.

The crisis in psychology has been articulated by Hughes (2018a) in identifying six broad crises facing psychology. He maintains that psychology as a discipline has been grappling with several interwoven crises for decades. He identified the following crisis:

- theoretical fragmentation (a paradigmatic crisis);
- reductionism (a measurement crisis);
- sloppy approaches to significance and effect sizes (a statistical crisis);
- a tendency to focus on a tiny sliver of the human population (a sampling crisis);

- premature optimism about the progress made by psychology, both in basic science and in resolving its reproducibility problems (an exaggeration crisis).

Hughes (2018b) claims that

> [j]ournals continue to prioritise statistically significant results over the reporting of null effects, thereby encouraging sloppy practices such as p-hacking and 'HARKing' (hypothesising after the results are known), and perpetuating the file-drawer [see following section] effect. Citations (and h-indexes) are still routinely used to assess the output of individual researchers even though everyone knows that such measures say nothing about (and so fail to promote) research quality. [The] persistence with using citations as a measure of researcher prowess encourages salami-slicing, gratuitous self-citation, and other destructive habits that serve to distort research.

However, Hughes provides a route towards a more robust science that is transparent, and critical for psychology's journey to recovery as a potential scientific enterprise.

Bias in research psychology

Bias in research is a common phenomenon, and it may occur either intentionally or unintentionally. Bias is being economical or deviation from the truth in research methodology including research design and implementation. Research biases have implications for the reliability and validity of study findings and falsification and misinterpretation of data can have important consequences for clinical interventions. Research bias range from the initial design to dissemination and publication. Figure 4.1 presents the types of research bias in psychology.

Design bias occurs when there is poor constructive alignment between purpose and methodology of research. In addition, the philosophy and worldview of the researcher influence the choice of research question and methodology. Selection bias refers to a situation when randomising the sample is not possible which leads to underrepresentation of your study population. The use of the wrong inclusion or exclusion criteria for selecting the sample population is a valid reason for selection bias. Confounding, sometimes referred to as confounding bias, is mostly described as a 'mixing' or 'blurring' of effects' (Grimes & Schulz, 2002). They are other additional variables that are neglected to be taken into account during the study. This seems to occur when a researcher tries to determine the effect of an exposure on the occurrence of a psychological condition but then actually measures the effect of another factor (cause). Confounding bias is regarded as undesirable, as it obscures the

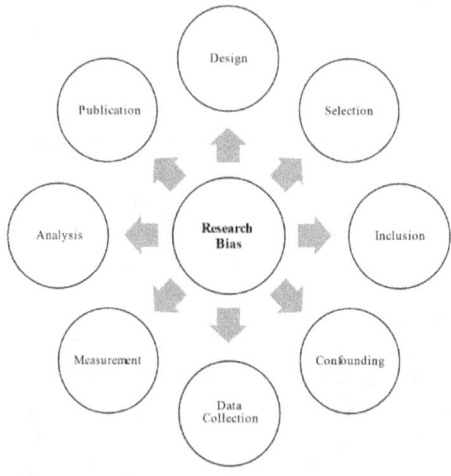

Figure 4.1 Types of research bias
Source: Adapted from Smith and Noble (2014).

'real' effect of an exposure, resulting in spurious conclusions. Both selection bias and confounding are present to some degree in all observational research.

Data collection, known as measurement bias, occurs in both qualitative and quantitative research methods. Being selective in the collection of data or using leading question in an interview may lead to introducing bias in the study. This result in the information being collected to be unrepresentative of the situation under study. Sources of bias can be prevented by carefully planning the data collection process. Measurement bias refers to the distorted measurement of key study variables and is present if a tool or instrument: has not been assessed for its psychometric properties (e.g., validity and reliability). Analysis bias may occur during data processing. When selecting and analysing the data, the researcher may naturally look for data that confirm his or her beliefs, thoughts, outcomes that favours the research hypothesis. A publication bias is a type of bias that refers to a situation where studies (Quantitative) with statistically significant findings are more likely to be published than those with negative findings. This type of bias is more likely to occur in in qualitative studies because of a lack of depth when describing study methodologies and findings are not clearly presented. Publication bias also relates as the tendency from authors to publish studies with significant results (Dickersin, 1990). The file-drawer effect is linked with the idea of publication bias and occurs when a large number of studies are undertaken but a minority of the studies that support the null hypothesis are placed in the file cabinets. Scargle (2000) argued that 'Statistical combination can be trusted only if it is known with certainty that all studies that have been carried out are included' (p. 91). One important bias that occurs in orientalist research is the issue of cultural bias including ethnocentrism and cultural relativism. Culture bias in psychology occurs when research studies are conducted in one culture in WEIRD countries and the findings are generalised and said to apply to lots of different cultures. Orientalist research with ingrained cultural bias is part of the colonisation and globalisation process.

Understanding research bias allows research psychologists to identify potential bias and how to minimise these biases. This is essential for the practice of evidence-based psychology. Students and research psychologists need to thoroughly scrutinise the design and methodology of the research; selecting a sample being representative of the research population (in quantitative studies, use probability sampling; in experiment, use random assignment); by gathering data from multiple sources; paying attention to data collection process and analysis; review the interpretation and analysis of data; and obtain review of the data and the discussion of the findings from your peers on an informal basis. It is also important, longitudinal studies to account for participants who withdraw (for known or unknown reason) during the study as this could bias your results. Triangulation (used of mixed on integrated research methods) to enhance the validity and credibility of the findings. Researchers have an ethical duty to outline the limitations of studies and account for potential sources of bias in the dissemination and publication of their study. The findings of robust research have implications for policy development in health provisions and delivery. In psychology research, there are also those Questionable Research Practices (QRS) which is prevalent in published research. These include HARKing, cherry-picking, P-hacking, fishing and data dredging or mining (Andrade, 2021) citation bias. Figure 4.2 presents the questionable research practices.

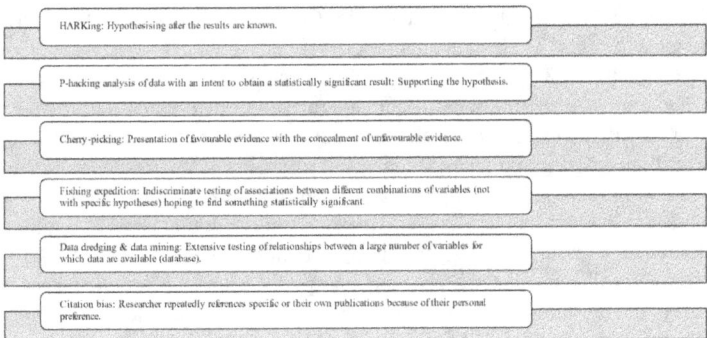

Figure 4.2 Questionable research practices in research
Source: Adapted from Andrade (2021).

Some of these QRS are applicable in the field of Islāmic psychology research. One of the Questionable Research Practices is the new trend of the creeping of "cherry-picking" in Islāmic psychology. That is presenting only one side of a narrative or give it disproportional covering (of their own works) while ignoring the facts or opinions that could support alternative viewpoints. This selective bias or 'cherry-picking' is used as a rhetoric technique to support their own point of new. For example, if you are an adherent of our school of thought, you will be acknowledged in the literature. This approach prevent good practice and evidence-based findings to be totally ignored in the literature. This is a deficit in scholarship in Islāmic psychology. It has been suggested that '[p]artialistic evidence that is marshalled to support a particular view, decision or approach, often leads to unintended outcomes and destroys the wholistic purposes (*maqasid*) that are desired, instead of contributing to their achievement' (Auda, 2021, p. 51). Andrade (2021) posits that the knowledge of questionable research practices should be disseminated so that students, researchers and readers understand what approaches to statistical analysis and reporting amount to scientific misconduct. In Islāmic psychology, there is a need to an openness to critical examination of the research work and the inherited knowledge from the classical and contemporary scholars.

Decolonising psychology research

It is becoming increasingly important for researchers to critically reflect on Western-oriented research approaches and outcomes due of its colonialist, Eurocentric and orientalist approaches. Decolonisation is about challenging the dominance of the Eurocentric and orientalist psychology epistemologies in research and knowledge production. There is now a growing global decolonisation movement which question various aspects of colonisation, Eurocentrism and 'Whiteness' psychology science (Adams et al., 2015, 2018; Bulhan, 2015; Dudgeon & Walker, 2015; Lacerda, 2015; Gómez-Ordóñez et al., 2021). How do we decolonise research methodologies?

Connell (2018) proposes two possible strategies for decolonising social science: (a) addressing what it studies, focusing on research and (b) how it proceeds, focusing on the methodology adopted (p. 6). In academic research, decolonisation takes a number of stages in its process. This is presented in Figure 4.3. An important first step in the process of decolonising psychology research is have a critical review of the dominant epistemology (knowledge about the reality); ontology (belief in what is real); axiology, moral and ethics; and research methodology (how to carry out the research based on epistemology). The four dimensions (epistemology, ontology axiology, and ethics) need to be deconstructed in order to shape and frame research studies with Muslims based on an Islāmic paradigm (philosophy and worldview).

Decolonisation, epistemological bias and limitations in psychology 55

Figure 4.3 Decolonising psychology research

This means challenging the nature, type and assumptions of research philosophy and ideologies in psychology research. This also about confronting long-standing biases and omissions that limit current orientalist research studies. This involve a paradigm shift and a fundamental reconsideration of what kinds of research should be undertaken, the research process itself and the type of methodology to be adopted. It has been suggested that the approaches in decolonising research methodologies are to 'contribute, facilitate and convene debates on complexities of decoloniality; Re-evaluate research funding flows; Consider the various world views imprinting incumbency [mostly Eurocentric] world views and philosophies; Document cases that challenge the normative; and articulate or customise systems facilitating research' (Ndege & Onyango, 2021).

However, there are several questions that need to be answered in the process of decolonising psychology research (University of Warwick, Education Studies, 2018):

- How do assumptions about power affect what we select as problems for research; who pays for this research; and what purposes does the research serve?
- What relationship does the researcher have with those being researched?

- Does the research have an action orientation?
- Who conducts the research?
- Are bodies of knowledge distorted?
- How is research methodology itself distorted by a dominant tradition?

It is important to remove the dominant epistemology, ontology, axiology and research methodology to enable the establishment of an indigenous research methodology that taking into context the questions as stated earlier and the cultural, political, social and religious environs of the population being investigated. This is a complex and long process in the elimination of the residual effects of colonisation ad globalisation. For a more comprehensive literature on the decolonisation process see Keane et al. (2017), Smith (2012), Wilson (2001), and Zavala (2013).

Conclusion

A more integrated research scholarship in Islāmic psychology of the twenty-first century, rather than being stuck in their colonial and orientalist past, would have Islāmic beliefs, ethics and values drive its development. We need to use our rich research scholarship and cross fertilisation of ideas and approaches that are cross-contextual from different school of thought to develop scholarship in Islāmic psychology research. Malkawi (2014) suggested that the classical Muslim scholars, despite their different school of thought, agreed that

> knowledge should be interconnected, complementary, and organically linked to the knowledge of God. In the view of these scholars, the fact that all sciences originate from a single divine source is the foundation for the ultimate integration and unity of knowledge.
>
> (p. 12)

This would liberate us from intellectual oppression and partialism from within and from the clutches of orientalism.

However, this is not to imply that the existing methodologies are not fit for purpose, but it means appreciating the benefits and limitations of existing methodologies in both Islāmic studies and psychology and articulating them to reflecting on the divine revelation. For Islāmic scholarship to emerge as a force 'majeure' in academic instructions, there is a need to challenge existing orientalist research methodologies in the social sciences, especially in psychology with the task of decolonising the orientalist philosophical, epistemological and ontological research approaches and methodologies. This is about dismantling and disconnecting the ways of knowing in research and knowledge production to overcome the 'epistemic privilege' of those dominant few that monopolise the authority of knowledge in the world.

References

Adams, G., Dobles, I., Gómez, L., Kurtiş, T., & Molina, L. E. (2015). Decolonizing psychological science: Introduction to the special thematic session. *Journal of Social and Political Psychology*, 3(1), 213–238.
Adams, G., Estrada-Villalta, S., & Gómez-Ordóñez, L. H. (2018). The modernity/coloniality of being: Hegemonic psychology as intercultural relations. *International Journal of Intercultural Relations*, 62, 13–22.
Andrade, C. (2021). HARKing, cherry-picking, p-hacking, fishing expeditions, and data dredging and mining as questionable research practices. *The Journal of Clinical Psychiatry*, 82(1), 20f13804.
Arnett, J. J. (2008). The neglected 95%: Why American psychology needs to become less American. *The American Psychologist*, 63(7), 602–614.
Auda, J. (2021). *Re-Envisioning Islamic Scholarship; Maqasid Methodology as a New Approach*. Swansea, UK: Claritas Books.
Awaad, R. (2021). The Father of Modern Islāmic Psychology: Dr Malik Badri's Legacy. TRT World. Retrieved from www.trtworld.com/opinion/the-father-of-modern-Islāmic-psychology-dr-malik-badri-s-legacy-44255.
Badri, M. B. (1979). *The Dilemma of Muslim Psychologists*. London: MWH London Publishers.
Bulhan, H. A. (2015). *Frantz Fanon and the Psychology of Oppression*. New York: Plenum Press.
Connell, R. (2018). Decolonizing sociology. *Contemporary Sociology*, 47(4), 399–407.
De Sousa Santos, B. (2010). *Epistemologias del sur*. Mexico: Siglo XX.
Dickersin, K. (1990). The existence of publication bias and risk factors for its occurrence. *JAMA*, 263(10), 1385–1389.
Dudgeon, P., & Walker, R. (2015). Decolonising Australian psychology: Discourse, strategies, and practice. *Journal of Social and Political Psychology*, 3(1), 276–297.
Gómez-Ordóñez, L.H., Adams, G., Ratele, K., Suffla, S., Stevens, G., & Reddy, G. (2021). Decolonising psychological science: Encounters and cartographies of resistance. *The Psychologist*, September, pp. 54–57.
Grimes, D. A., & Schulz, K. F. (2002). Bias and causal associations in observational research. *Lancet (London, England)*, 359(9302), 248–252.
Grosfoguel, R. (2013). Epistemic Racism/Sexism, Westernized Universities and the Four Genocides/Epistemicides of the Long 16th Century. *Human Architecture: Journal of the Sociology of Self-Knowledge*, I(1), 73–90.
Henrich, J., Heine, S. J., & Norenzayan, A. (2010). The weirdest people in the world? *The Behavioral and Brain Sciences*, 33(2–3), 61–135.
Hughes, B. M. (2018a). *Psychology in Crisis*. London: Palgrave.
Hughes, B. M. (2018b). *Psychology Is Still in Crisis*. Psychology Today. Retrieved from www.psychologytoday.com/us/blog/homeostasis-disruptor/201809/psychology-is-still-in-crisis.
Ibn Majah. *Sunan Ibn Majah 3994*. In-book reference: Book 36, Hadith 69. English translation: Vol. 5, Book 36, Hadith 3994. Hasan (Darussalam).
Keane, M., Khupe, C., & Seehawer, M. (2017). Decolonising methodology: Who benefits from indigenous knowledge research? *Educational Research for Social Change (ERSC)*, 6(1), 12–24.
Kirmayer, L. J., & Minas, I. H. (2000). The future of cultural psychiatry: An international perspective. *Canadian Journal of Psychiatry*, 45(5), 438–446.

Klenke, K. (2008). *Qualitative Research in the Study of Leadership.* Leeds, UK: Emerald Group Publishing.

Lacerda, F. (2015). Insurgency, theoretical decolonization and social decolonization: Lessons from Cuban psychology. *Journal of Social and Political Psychology*, 3(1), 298–323.

Lawson, R. B., Graham, J. E., & Baker, K. M. (2007). Contemporary psychology: Global forces. In R. B. Lawson, J. E. Graham, & K. M. Baker (Eds.), *A History of Psychology: Globalization, Ideas, and Applications* (1st ed.). New York: Routledge.

Machery, E. (2010). Explaining why experimental behavior varies across cultures: A missing step in "the weirdest people in the world?". *Behavioral and Brain Sciences*, 33(2–3), 101–102.

Malkawi, F. H. (2014). *Epistemological Integration: Essentials of an Islāmic Methodology.* Translated from the Arabic by Nancy Roberts. Herndon, VA: International Institute of Islāmic Thought.

Mignolo, W. (2010). Introduction: Coloniality of power and de-colonial thinking. In W. Mignolo & A. Escobar (Eds.), *Globalisation and the Decolonial Option* (pp. 1–21). New York: Routledge.

Ndege, N., & Onyango, J. (2021). How do we 'decolonise' research methodologies? *Africa Research and Impact Network/African Centre for Technology Studies.* Retrieved from https://steps-centre.org/blog/how-do-we-decolonise-research-methodologies/.

Ndlovu-Gatsheni, S. J. (2013a). *Empire, Global Coloniality and African Subjectivity.* Oxford: Berghahn Books.

Ndlovu-Gatsheni, S. J. (2013b). *Coloniality of Power in Postcolonial Africa.* Dakar: CODESRIA.

Open Science Collaboration. (2015). Psychology. Estimating the reproducibility of psychological science. *Science* (New York, N.Y.), 349(6251), aac4716. https://doi.org/10.1126/science.aac4716.

Scargle, J. D. (2000). Publication bias: The "file-drawer" problem in scientific inference. *Journal of Scientific Exploration*, 14(1), 91–106.

Shaikh, A. (2023). Relevance of research methodologies used in health psychology for British Muslims: An epistemological critique on the colonisation of knowledge production. In S. Dogra (Ed.), *British Muslims, Ethnicity and Health Inequalities.* Edinburgh: Edinburgh University Press.

Smith, J., & Noble, H. (2014). Bias in research. *Evidence-Based Nursing*, 17(4), 100–101.

Smith, L. (2012). *Decolonizing Methodologies: Research and Indigenous Peoples.* London: Zed Books.

University of Warwick, Education Studies. (2018). *What Is Decolonising Methodology?* Retrieved from https://warwick.ac.uk/fac/soc/ces/research/current/socialtheory/maps/decolonising/.

Wilson, C. (2001). Decolonizing methodologies. *Social Policy Journal of New Zealand*, 17, 214–217.

Zavala, M. (2013). What do we mean by decolonizing research strategies? Lessons from decolonizing, indigenous research projects in New Zealand and Latin America. *Decolonization: Indigeneity, Education & Society*, 2(1), 55–71.

5 Integrated research methodology and research framework in Islāmic psychology

Introduction

The Islāmisation of knowledge development has stressed the importance of both the epistemological (theoretical content of human thought) and the methodological dimensions (research) approaches in knowledge integration. Muslim researchers and scholars have two approaches or methodologies in studying human behaviours and experiences. The first method is the use of intuition, empirical and rational based on the Western paradigm. However, this research methodology does not recognise divine Islāmic revelation as a proper source of scientific knowledge, and espoused Eurocentric values and culture. In contrast, the alternative methodology of research is to adopt the methodology of the classical Muslim scholars and contemporary thinkers based on the *Tawhîdic* paradigm and the Islāmic worldview. This chapter focuses on an examination of integrated research and guidelines in undertaking research in Islāmic psychology.

Integrated research methodology

Research methodology are specific procedures for collecting and analysing data and these processes are based on the type of research question and design. Research methods are qualitative which focuses on concepts, subjective experiences, themes, wordings and ideas and while quantitative research deals aims at crunching numbers and the application of statistics. For a comprehensive account of the aims and focus of qualitative, quantitative or both (see Rassool, 2023, p. 179). Both quantitative and qualitative research methodologies are used in Islāmic psychology. Figure 5.1 summarises the Islāmic traditions in research scholarship.

The notion of knowledge integration in research from an Islāmic perspective is to integrate Islāmic ethics and epistemological values in social sciences, including Islāmic psychology. Kasule (2015) maintains that knowledge integration 'involves integrating Islāmic moral and epistemological values in

DOI: 10.4324/9781003346241-5

60 Integrated research methodology and research framework

Figure 5.1 Islāmic traditions in research scholarship
Source: Adapted from Akhmetova and Rafikov (2022).

the various disciplines of knowledge that are taught' (p. 124). It has been suggested that

> [i]n the context of research from an Islāmic perspective, it is the process of synthesising research methodologies and approaches (empirical, rational) with Islāmic sciences methodologies. Both knowledge integration' and integrated research focus on the integration of empirical evidence ('*Ilm 'aqli*') with revealed knowledge ('*Ilm 'naqli*), and the synthesis of both sources of knowledge into an integrated model based on *Tawhîdic* paradigm.
> (Rassool, 2023, p. 175)

The essence here is to bring knowledge from the different perspectives and sources under one umbrella to achieve a purpose or a set of goals. In integrated research methodology, there is no conflicting knowledge between the revealed knowledge from the Qur'ān and *Sunnah* ('*Ilm 'naqli*) and the rational knowledge ('*Ilm 'aqli*) based on intuition, human intellect, observation and experimentation. In essence, the revealed knowledge is used to study exclusively matters of ethics and morality and in contrast, rational knowledge is used to answer questions of an empirical nature. However, the transmitted knowledge requires the guidance of '*Ilm naqli* regarding fundamentals like 'objectivity (*Istiqamat*), ethics (*Akhlāq*), and purposiveness (*Gha'iyyat*)' (Kasule, 2015). Figure 5.2 depicts the integrated research methodology in Islāmic psychology.

Integrated research methodology and research framework 61

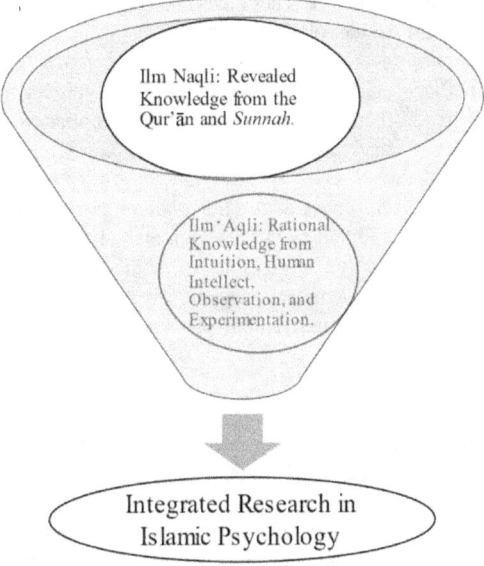

Figure 5.2 Integrated research methodology in Islāmic psychology

In Islāmic research methodology, there is also the need to exercise *Ijtihād* (independent reasoning). Ijtihad has always been an important tool and source for Muslims to resolve psychosocial issues and its use as a methodology has been a significant process in the development of Islāmic thoughts and knowledge. According to Imam Al-Ghazālī, *Ijtihād* means to expand once capacity in certain matter and use it to the utmost (Cited in Aboobackaer, 2019).

The task of developing an integrated methodology of research in Islāmic psychology should have a fourfold aim. Rassool (2023) has proposed that:

First, the new methodology should include Qur'ān and *Sunnah* as the primary source of knowledge. Secondly, the methodologies of the Islāmic traditions should also be used as a paradigm by Muslim psychologists and scholars should proceeded to develop research methodologies in Islāmic psychology. The use of historical works from Islāmic classical scholars and work from contemporary scholars are also sources of psychology knowledge. Thirdly, we need to use both qualitative and quantitative methodologies of research which provide a holistic and multidisciplinary approach. Fourthly, the desired methodology must allow the integration of both revealed knowledge and knowledge from quantitative and qualitative research methodologies.

(p. 196)

62 Integrated research methodology and research framework

In addition, Muslim research psychologists should experiment in the integration of the Maqasid Methodology (Auda, 2021) in the integrated research approach. The purpose of an integrated research approach (qualitative and quantitative methodologies) is that it provides both a vertical and horizontal understanding of the theme under investigation, it produces potential convergent outcomes or divergent outcomes, and it is applicable to the type of research used in Islāmic psychology. The application of an integrated research method exploits the robustness of the quantitative and qualitative methods while neutralising the limitations of each approach. The purpose and rationale in the use of quantitative and qualitative methods should be delineated. In Islāmic psychology, to generate a hypothesis a qualitative approach can be used and the use of quantitative approach for hypothesis testing. Rassool (2023) suggests that there are

> Two ways of using the two methods: sequentially or in parallel. The sequential approach of the combined methodologies follows a purposeful, staged approach. At the initial stage, a quantitative methodology may be use followed by a qualitative study (stage 2) or vice versa. This would depend on the context, purpose and design of the research. In the parallel approach both methodologies are used . For example, a large survey may be accompanied by a focus group.
>
> (pp. 197–198)

For those who wish to apply the integrated methodology, they need to have a sound knowledge and develop research skills in both methodologies and in the Maqasid Methodology. Figure 5.3 presents the framework for conducting integrated research in Islāmic psychology.

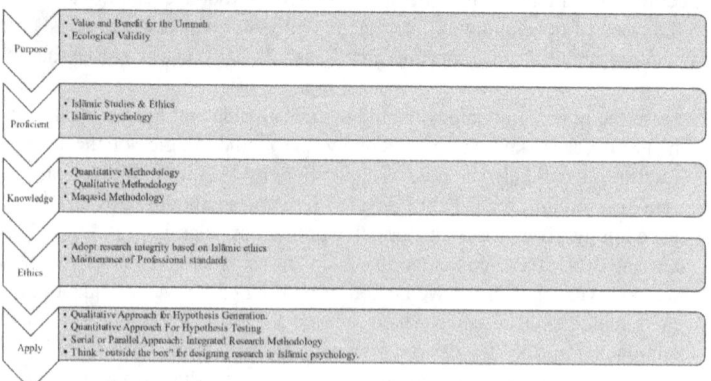

Figure 5.3 Framework for conducting integrated research

Integrated research methodology and research framework 63

Framework for undertaking research in Islāmic psychology

An overview of the literature (Dar al-Iftaa Al-Missriyyah, 2022) focusing on different guidelines in undertaking research in Islāmic studies is presented. The framework have been adapted for research in Islāmic psychology and is presented in Figure 5.4. The framework is presented in a linear fashion, but it does not mean that the guidelines are utilised in a sequential way. The guidelines presented are adapted depending on the nature and process of research. Having good intention (*niyyah*) is a prerequisite for any research in Islāmic psychology. The guidelines the framework include ecological validity, research competence, mapping the research field, literature review, understanding the texts and meanings, scholarly integrity in relating ideas, and impartial and honest criticism.

Ecological validity

The purpose of research in the field of Islāmic psychology should have benefits and should bring value to humanity, thus, deemed to have 'ecological validity.' Ecological validity in Islāmic psychology refers to the extent to which the theme of the research and findings can be beneficial to humankind and the environment, and applicable to real-life settings. For a research activity that consume wasted time and resources and offers no benefit is itself problematic. In Islāmic traditions, the classical scholars when asked about rulings or the details of an issue, they would respond

> [i]s this an actually existing issue? Research outcomes should benefit society and the discovering of new ways of improving people's health and

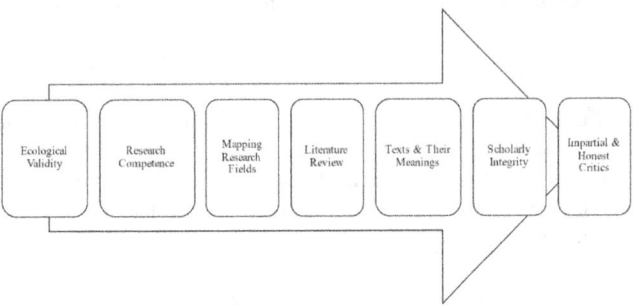

Figure 5.4 Phases of undertaking research
Source: Adapted from Dar al-Iftaa Al-Missriyyah (2022).

socio-economic conditions. This is an indication of the strong connection between knowledge gained from research and deriving human benefits and the importance of authentic knowledge from the Qur'ān and *Sunnah* in guiding people.

Research competence

There are two conditions attached to this category research competence and preparation for research. The researcher must be acquainted and have a good grounding of the Qur'ān and the *Sunnah*, basic Arabic language and Islāmic psychology. This is reflected in the following *Hadīth*. Ibrahim b. 'Abd ar-Rahman al-'Udhri reported God's messenger (ﷺ) as saying, 'In every successive century those who are reliable authorities will preserve this knowledge, rejecting the changes made by extremists, the plagiarisms of those who make false claims for themselves, and the interpretations of the ignorant' (Mishkat al-Masabih). This means that authentic knowledge of the Book of Allāh will be carried by the trustworthy ones in every time. It is important to rely on the Qur'ān and the *Sunnah* first as your primary sources of truth. The researcher must also be well grounded in the Maqasid Methodology (Auda, 2021), research methodology in psychology, in both quantitative and qualitative or in integrated or mixed methodologies. What is observed in the Islāmic literature and research in Islāmic psychology is the lack of knowledge of the Qur'ān, *Sunnah* and Islāmic studies. The following statement echoes these sentiments:

> We observed their inadequacy in their work by randomly pick out verses from the Qur'ān or *Hadīth* narrations and derive explanations or rulings that does not conform to existing commentary (*Tafsir*) of the Qur'ān. Those authors or researchers usually misuse verses from the Qur'ān as evidence to support their opinions or findings, without referring the context the verses are used and a proper understanding of *Tafsir*.
>
> (cited in in Dar al-Iftaa Al-Missriyyah, 2022)

This observation is common in websites relating to Islāmic psychology or Islām in general.

Ibn Sirin (n.d.) said '[t]his knowledge is a religion, so consider from whom you receive your religion.' It is narrated by 'Abdullah bin Amr: I heard the Prophet (ﷺ) saying

> Allāh will not deprive you of knowledge after he has given it to you, but it will be taken away through the death of the religious learned men with their knowledge. Then there will remain ignorant people who, when

Integrated research methodology and research framework 65

consulted, will give verdicts according to their opinions whereby they will mislead others and go astray.

Bukhari (a)

The lack of adequate preparation of Muslim psychologists in Islāmic studies and psychology is impending scholarship in the development of Islāmic thought. So, the preparation for research, with the right intention and having competence in the Qur'ān, the *Sunnah* and research methodologies are the upmost priority.

It is incumbent on every researcher to have acquired the fundamental knowledge in psychology and in Islāmic psychology with sound research skills. The researcher should be acquainted with the literature the methods of conducting research, research design, research frameworks, sampling procedures, measurement and format of research reports. While researchers may use intuition, authority, rationalism and empiricism to generate new theory of knowledge. However, the scientific method can only be used to address empirical questions, the researchers also need to master earlier classical works on the science of the soul (*Ilm an Nafs*) and research traditions in Islāmic studies. Ibn Khaldun (n.d.) stated that

> [p]roficiency and mastery in a field is only achieved by obtaining a skill in comprehending the principles and rules of the field, and understanding its problems, and deriving solution from its principles. As long as this skill is not obtained, proficiency in that field will not be obtained.
> (Cited in in Dar al-Iftaa Al- Missriyyah, 2022)

The competence in research is of the upmost importance as '[h]e should possess good qualities of concentration, patience, passion, curiosity, critical mind, dedication and other qualities related to that aspect' (Dalhat, 2015, p. 150). The researcher in Islāmic psychology should be re-oriented in knowledge of the Islāmic worldview with the understanding and comprehension that 'Allāh is the primary source of true knowledge, how the state of the heart [*qalb*] impacts receiving and utilising knowledge, and how knowledge (*'ilm*) is connected to a complex web of fundamental meanings' (Auda, 2021, p. 71). Developing reflective skills is a valuable tool for the researcher in the cycles of reflection of the Qur'ān and the *Sunnah*.

Mapping the research field

In the field of *Hadīth* and jurisprudence, scholars have explained the importance of proper structuring and mapping of the research field. 'They call it in Arabic '*Al-sabr wa'l-taqseem.*'

In Islāmic psychology, mapping may be used as a methodological research strategy. Concept map has also primarily been used as a means to assess knowledge integration (Besterfield-Sacre et al., 2004). A concept map 'is a schematic device for representing a set of concept meanings embedded in a framework of propositions' (Novak & Gowin, 2022, p. 15). Daley (2004) suggested:

> Concept maps are created with the broader, more inclusive concepts at the top of the hierarchy, connecting through linking words with other concepts than can be subsumed. Concept maps are an important strategy in qualitative inquiry because they help the researcher focus on meaning. The maps support researchers in their attempts to make sure that qualitative data is embedded in a particular context.

In this context, a concept map can be used as a visual representation of the relationships between various factors or concepts of the research, provides a framework for a research project, provides a synthesis of the data, analyses relationships of themes and interconnections in a study and has a means of presenting the findings of a research. A mind map may also be used, as identified in the Maqasid Methodology, when a researcher through the cycles of reflection tabulate all knowledge that is directly or potentially relevant to the purpose of the research.

Literature review

The literature review is the beginning of any purposeful research on a particular theme. This is a critical appraisal of the landscape of the subject and for placing research findings into context. Unfortunately, students of psychology tend to produce a description of the literature rather than a critical appraisal of the research findings, including the limitations of previous research on the subjects. The sources of the literature review include the Qur'ān; *Hadith*; and digital access to research papers, academic texts, review articles and databases. It should be noted that '[r]esearchers must exercise caution, for knowledge of the value of any given source is very important for helping arrive at the truth' (Dar al-Iftaa Al-Missriyyah, 2022). The task of a literature review is to make a critical review of the literature and build an argument or statement of the problem. The writing of a literature review requires a range of skills including collection, identification, evaluation, critical examination and summarisation of peer-reviewed published data into a cohesive and informative unbiased narrative. It has been suggested that

> there is no way to construct a framework of contemporary reality without drawing on literature, classical and contemporary, as well as drawing on the researcher's perception and experience of reality. Identifying

Integrated research methodology and research framework

suitable primary and secondary sources of information is therefore very important, as well as ways of perceiving and assessing the realities at hand.

(Auda, 2021, p. 123)

The collection and review of the existing literature should be presented in a systematic way thoroughly analysing the intellectual material, its ordering and framework so as to produce a framework of contemporary reality. This part also relates to the previous statement in relation to the evaluation or critical examination of the literature. In the context of Islāmic studies or Islāmic psychology,

> Each issue should be prefaced by a Qur'ānic passage and a sound prophetic report. There should also be an exegesis [explanation]of these texts from reliable sources. This methodology clarifies for us the development of thinking of the people of knowledge, their status, and what they have contributed over generations. From this, we may come to realise the impact of time and place.

(Dar al-Iftaa Al-Missriyyah, 2022)

Understanding the texts and meanings

This is appropriate and relevant to both Islāmic studies and Islāmic psychology. The danger in Islāmic psychology is that a scholar or researcher follows his own ideology and subjective notions in the dissemination of knowledge. Hassan (2022) noted that in Islāmic psychology and counselling 'people are marshalling themselves to offer what is Islāmic and what is not without the requisite tools and knowledge [of the Qur'ān and Sunnah]. That is why the Qur'ān has warned against falsehood.

وَلَا تَقُولُواْ لِمَا تَصِفُ أَلْسِنَتُكُمُ ٱلْكَذِبَ هَٰذَا حَلَٰلٌ وَهَٰذَا حَرَامٌ لِّتَفْتَرُواْ عَلَى ٱللَّهِ ٱلْكَذِبَ ۚ إِنَّ ٱلَّذِينَ يَفْتَرُونَ عَلَى ٱللَّهِ ٱلْكَذِبَ لَا يُفْلِحُونَ

- *And do not say about what your tongues assert of untruth, This is lawful, and this is unlawful, to invent falsehood about Allāh. Indeed, those who invent falsehood about Allāh will not succeed.*

(An-Nahl 16:116, interpretation of the meaning)

It is narrated by 'Abdullah bin 'Amr bin Al-'As that the Prophet stated (ﷺ):

> Allāh does not take away the knowledge, by taking it away from (the hearts of) the people but takes it away by the death of the religious learned men till when none of the (religious learned men) remains, people will take as

their leaders' ignorant persons who when consulted will give their verdict without knowledge. So, they will go astray and will lead the people astray. (Bukhari (b)).

Imam Malik (1983) (may Allāh be pleased with him) remarked: 'Whoever is asked about a religious matter, before responding he should imagine both Heaven and Hell before him and consider his outcome in the Hereafter. Only then should he respond.' The problems which this inauthentic knowledge is that it is based on weak arguments, deviant opinions and explanation of the text. On this topic, Ibn Hazm al-Andalusi (1985), the great polymath, said:

> There is nothing more harmful to knowledge and its people than those who enter into it, yet are not from it. They are ignorant, but think they are knowledgeable; they cause corruption while they think they are rectifying matters.
>
> (p. 24)

In sum, we need to be objective and neutral and rely on authentic text. Due to the nature of research in a multidisciplinary field, it would be essential to consult specialist who are an authority in the area of study. That is taking information from trustworthy original sources. For example, in Islāmic studies or Islāmic psychology, the researcher needs to consult specialists in the field who have a sound understanding of methodological framework and not 'wannabe' scholar. In summary, the references or interpretation of the text and their meaning should be from trustworthy original sources, and specialists in the subject of the text should be given prominence.

Scholarly integrity in relating ideas

Muslim researchers should adhere to the Qur'ānic concept of integrity when relating and attributing ideas to people. Qadi 'Iyad (n.d.) stated that

> [s]cholarly integrity in attributing sayings and ideas to people is to be done without even the slightest shortcoming, whether the attribution is to a great person or not, to a Muslim or not, to a pious person or not, to an early personality or a later one.
>
> (Cited in Dar al-Iftaa Al-Missriyyah, 2022)

In Islāmic psychology, researchers should adhere to the Islāmic ethical principles in addition to the professional standards essential for the responsible practice of research. The concept of ethical competence can be defined

> in terms of character strength, ethical awareness, moral judgement skills and willingness to do good. Virtuous professional, experience of a

professional, human communication, ethical knowledge and supporting surroundings in the organisation can be seen as prerequisites for ethical competence.

(Kulju et al., 2016, p. 401).

Islāmic ethical issues are examined in Chapter 3.

Adhering to those principles goes beyond the attributing ideas and theory to previous scholars but also implementing the principles of the Islāmic Ethics (*akhlaq*) which is derived from the Qur'ān and *Sunnah*. The characteristics of the researcher include truth, integrity, honesty, fairness, disclosure of conflicts of interest and care and protection of human subjects and animals in the conduct of research. In addition, the researcher should not engage in unscholarly behaviour in plagiarised texts from other authors or omitting authors who do not share the same ideologies as the author and also omitting parts, so as to remove disagreements with the point of view of the researcher. It has been suggested that

> [t]he scholars of Islām have set a great example in such scholarly integrity because the Qur'ān itself has laid down this principle. This is of great benefit in the Islāmic sciences, like the science of *Hadīth*, which has set out a methodology for authentic reports narrated from the Prophe (☙)t
>
> (Dar al-Iftaa Al-Missriyyah, 2022)

There is no doubt that the same some be applicable to Islāmic psychology.

Impartial and honest criticism

It is important provide impart and honest criticism without creating violations of professional behaviours. Accordingly, the accomplished and trained researcher 'has the right to understand and explain his own understanding of the Qur'ān, *Sunnah* and deriving intellectual production from them. He has the right to criticise and evaluate constructively' (Dar al-Iftaa Al-Missriyyah, 2022). The principle for this right to evaluate is found in the golden statement of Imam Malik bin Anas , 'Everyone's opinion may be accepted or rejected except for the person in this grave,' pointing to the grave of the Prophet (☙) . This is because in the Islāmic paradigm only the Messenger of Allāh (☙) is infallible. However, the self-criticism should start with the researcher or scholar as well providing constructive criticisms to the works of other scholars. As the scholars would say, 'Beware of putting forth your works before they have been refined and looked over many times' (cited in (Dar al-Iftaa Al-Missriyyah, 2022).

In summary, it is valuable for the researcher or scholar in Islāmic psychology to engage with the Islāmic traditions in scholarship and research and have a good comprehension of the methodologies. Understanding of the texts of the

Qur'ān and *Sunnah* is crucial in any research in Islāmic psychology. However, the Qur'ān and *Sunnah* should be used as a primary source of knowledge because of their absolute truth. Finally, the aim of the scholar is to identify and explain these truths (or proofs) which are revealed in the text and the natural world. Islāmic research methodology should be anchored on Islāmic philosophy comprising components such as Islāmic worldview, Islāmic epistemology and Islāmic ontology.

Conclusion

The paradigm of scientific research consists of ontology, epistemology methodology and methods based on revealed knowledge and empirical evidence. The worldviews of Muslims play a vital role in research process and in designing purpose of the research. According to Shafii (1985)

> The task of integration is . . . rather a systematic reorientation and restructuring of the entire field of human knowledge in accordance with a new set of criteria and categories, derived from, and based on [the] Islāmic worldview.
>
> (p. 6)

It is the Islāmic research philosophy that drives the philosophical position of a researcher and embedded with the Islāmic worldview. It is those two mega framework that have significant influence the research questions, methodology and interpretation of findings. In this context, the integrated research method combined with the Maqasid Methodology provides a robust Islāmic scholarship in research. Research scholarship in Islām is based on the identifying and disseminating the absolute truth which can be found in divine revelation and the universe and is governed by the *Tawhīd* paradigm

References

Aboobackaer, A. A. (2019). *Institution of Ijtihad and Modern World.* Retrieved from www.researchgate.net/profile/Anas-Aboobackaer.

Akhmetova, E., & Rafikov, I. (2021). *Course on Methodology of Scientific Research and Concept Formation (ITKI 6001).* Institute of Integrated Knowledge. Retrieved from http://ikiacademy.org.

Auda, J. (2021). *Re-envisioning Islāmic Scholarship: Maqasid Methodology as a New Approach.* Swansea: Claritas Publishing House.

Besterfield-Sacre, M., Gerchak, J., Lyons, M., Shuman, L. J., & Wolfe, H. (2004). Scoring concept maps: An integrated rubric for assessing. *Journal of Engineering Education*, 93(2), 105–115.

Bukhari (a). *Sahih al-Bukhari 7307.* In-book reference: Book 96, Hadith 38. USC-MSA web (English) reference: Vol. 9, Book 92, Hadith 410.

Integrated research methodology and research framework 71

Bukhari (b). *Sahih al-Bukhari 100*. In-book reference: Book 3, Hadith 42. USC-MSA web (English) reference: Vol. 1, Book 3, Hadith 100.

Daley, B. J. (2004). *Concept Maps: Theory, Methodology*. Technology Proc. of the First Int. Conference on Concept Mapping Pamplona, Spain. Retrieved from http://cmc.ihmc.us/Papers/cmc2004-060.pdf.

Dalhat, Y. (2015). Introduction to research methodology in Islamic studies. *Journal of Islamic Studies and Culture*, 3(2), 147–152.

Dar al-Iftaa Al-Missriyyah. (2022). *The Research Methodology in Traditional Islāmic Scholarship*. Retrieved from www.dar-alifta.org/foreign/ViewArticle.aspx?ID=113.

Hassan, A. (2022). *Hijacking of the Minbar*. Personal Communication.

Ibn Hazm al-Andalusi. (1985). *Al-Akhlaq wa'l-Siyar*. Beirut: Dar al-Kutub al-'Ilmiyyah.

Ibn Khaldun. (n.d.). Cited in Dar al-Ifta Al-Missriyyah (2022). *The Research Methodology in Traditional Islamic Scholarship*. Retrieved from www.dar-alifta.org/foreign/ViewArticle.aspx?ID=113.

Imam Malik. (1983). Cited in Qadi *'Iyad, Tartib al-Mudarik* (Vol. 1, p. 144). Saudi Arabia: Wizarat al-Awqaf wa'l-Shu'un al – Islamiyyah.

Kasule, O. H. (2015). Integration of knowledge (IOK) and textbook writing for Islāmic universities. *International Journal of Islāmic Thoughts*, 4(1), 123–126.

Kulju, K., Stolt, M., Suhonen, R., & Leino-Kilpi, H. (2016). Ethical competence: A concept analysis. *Nursing Ethics*, 23(4), 401–412.

Mishkat al-Masabih 248. In-book reference: Book 2, Hadith 44. Sahih (authentic) according to Ahmad Ibn Hanbal.

Novak, J.D., & Gowin, D.B. (2022). *Learning How to Learn*. New York: Cambridge University Press.

Qadi 'Iyad. (n.d.). Dar al-Ifta Al-Missriyyah (2022). *The Research Methodology in Traditional Islamic Scholarship*. Retrieved from www.dar-alifta.org/foreign/ViewArticle.aspx?ID=113.

Rassool, G. H. (2023). Research methodology in Islāmic psychology. In G. H. Rassool (ed.), *Islāmic Psychology: The Basics* (pp. 174–199). Oxford: Routledge.

Shafii, M. (1985). *Freedom from the Self: Sufism, Meditation, and Psychotherapy*. New York: Human Sciences Press.

6 Islāmic scholarship in research

An overview of the Maqasid Methodology

Introduction

This chapter provides an overview of the new Islāmic scholarship in research based on the Maqasid Methodology. It focuses on the limitations of past and current methodological Islāmic research scholarship and examines Maqasid Methodology Framework. The contents of this chapter is based on the book of Jasser Auda (2021), who introduced a new method of research in Islāmic Scholarship based on the Islāmic or Qur'ânic worldview. The primary goal of this intellectual Islāmic discourse is to 'revive the original concepts of Islāmic approach/ framework/ worldview in today's context' (p. 19). The essence of this research framework, based on the positioning of the Qur'ân and the *Sunnah* as the ultimate sources of knowledge, with an interconnected webs of meaning provides an integrative and holistic frame of reference for Islāmic scholars to integrate their diverse fields of knowledge. This is reflected in the broad definition Maqasid Methodology 'as a systematic approach in which connectivity, wholism and emergence are focal points' (Najimudeen, n.d.).

This new method of research in Islāmic Scholarship is based on the notion of 'purposeful connectivity.' That is

> Allāh Almighty created this universe in a connected and webbed fashion on all levels. He ordered humanity to preserve these connections and called severing them corruption on earth. These universal interconnections are not purposeless but rather, ordained for the achievements of the highest wisdoms and objectives on all levels. Therefore, a true Maqasid Methodology is essentially a methodology that integrates, looks towards the future and critiques based on the fulfilment of the purposes of connections or the lack thereof."
>
> (Auda, 2022, p. i)

Limitations of Islāmic scholarship

Auda (2021) was critical of current methodological research approaches to Islāmic scholarship by highlighting their limitations. He identified five

Islāmic scholarship in research 73

limitations in contemporary approaches to Islāmic scholarship: imitation (*taqlid*), partialism (*tajzi*), apologism (*tabrir*), contradiction (*tanaqud*) and deconstructionism (*tafkik*). In relation to imitation (*taqlid*), in Islāmic scholarship, this means that 'the blind imitation of the Islāmic heritage without reference to the Revelation versus utilising criteria from the Revelation to critique the Islāmic intellectual history in a nuanced and balanced way' (Auda, 2022, p. ii). This means that contemporary scholarships in Islāmic studies blindly promote historical opinions instead of using revelation as a primary source of knowledge. There is also the methodological limitation due to partialism (*tajzi*) which result in the fragmentation of knowledge and the absence of 'promoting synergy and integration between evidences, disciplines and specialisations' (p. ii).

Apologism (*tabrir*) in Islāmic scholarship

> especially in their classical form of the preservation of essentials, have been used extensively to justify pre-existing laws, systems, theories and frameworks associated with many human activities. Too often, application of the classical Maqasid to contemporary fields and disciplines including governance, social justice, economics, politics and culture betrays its original mandate by unquestioningly endorsing the status quo.
> (Auda, 2021, p. 60)

That is adopting an apologetic approach in the defence of a doctrine of the Higher Objectives of the *Shari'ah* without recourse to '*Shar'iah*-based restraints (*dawabit*). In these forms, the objectives are used to justify behaviours, laws, institutions and systems that actually betray the Islāmic objectives' (p. 60). Contradiction (*tanaqud*) occurs in the employment two bodies of knowledge that are not congruent with each other in the context of Islāmic beliefs and worldview. Auda (2021) ascribed this as a form of 'epistemological schizophrenia' (p. 60). Auda (2021) suggested that '[d]econstructionism in disciplines does not spring from an Islāmic foundation but rather from the post-modern, deconstructionist philosophy' (p. 63). This is in effect an elimination of divine revelation from the source of knowledge.

> It does that by placing the Words of Allāh and human literature and culture on the same plane. Some deconstructionist streams totally deny the authority of the Revelation on human life and consider the Qur'ān to be a mere 'cultural product' of its place and time.
> (Auda, 2021, p. 64)

Table 6.1 presents a tentative attempt at exploring the limitations of Islāmic psychology scholarship based on the limitations of the categories of imitation, partialism, apologism, contradiction and deconstructionism.

Table 6.1 Limitations of Islāmic psychology scholarship

Types of limitations	Examples in Islāmic psychology scholarship
Imitation	• Imitation of Freudian's Seminal Theory (Id, Ego and Super ego) equating with *nafs-e-ammārah, nafs-e-lawwāmah* and *nafs-e-muṭma'innah*. • In research, the use of descriptive or documentary approaches and the absence of direct reference to the Qur'ān and *Sunnah*.
Partialism	• This is a kind of 'epistemic partialist' research or the literature which involves being positively biased towards one school of thought in Islāmic beliefs and practices. • This is the use of preferential literature or one's own literature in research than is warranted by the evidence. • Partialistic evidence that is marshalled to support a particular view, decision or approach, often leads to unintended outcomes and destroys the wholistic purposes (*maqasid*) that are desired, instead of contributing to their achievement (Auda, 2021, p. 51). • Contemporary literature on Islāmic psychology fails to expose to differences of opinion and ways of dealing with disagreement.
Apologism	• Apologism in Islāmic psychology whereby the objectives, concepts and values of deviant sects and their innovations that involve beliefs and words that go against the Qur'ān are adopted. This is not in accordance with the Creed of *Ahl-us-Sunnah wa'l-Jamaa'ah*.
Contradiction	• In Islāmic psychology, there is contradiction that manifests in the integration of deep healing; Sufi's deep conscious breathing; breathing cycles of earth, water, fire, air and ether; emotional releases; reiki; yoga; reflexology, hypnotherapy; and Buddhist's mindfulness into the of therapeutic interventions. • 'This is an attempt to integrate two bodies of knowledge that do not emanate from the same basic beliefs and worldview' (Auda, 2021, p. 60).
Deconstructionism	• Islamic Liberation Psychology challenges unjust interpretations of Islam, drawing from Christian-based liberation theology. Ahl al-Sunnah wa'l-Jamaa'ah opposes it, safeguarding traditional interpretations to prevent deviation and potential conflicts with faith principles (Rassool, 2022).

Stages of the new Maqasid Methodology

Auda (2021) cautioned the researchers that this new Maqasid Methodology in itself

> will not address the researcher's specific inquiry. Instead, it will direct the scholar to the most suitable steps, content, meanings, emphases, connections and references that must be considered given their purpose or question. The methodology guides the researcher's analysis of particulars and generalities, and how the Revelation shifts seamlessly between the two.
> (p. 102)

Islāmic scholarship in research 75

In order to apply the different stages of the Maqasid Methodology in the research process, the researcher need to be re-oriented with the three most fundamental aspects of this re-orientation are (1) knowledge (*ilm*), (2) reality (*waqi*) and (3) scholarship (*ijtihad*). It has been pointed out that

> The dimensions related to knowledge in the Islāmic worldview are: its source, its logic and conceptualisations. Awareness of the reality includes the dimensions of assessing past and present and planning for the future. Scholarship, the role of which is to translate knowledge into an impact on the reality, includes the dimensions of its scope, scholars and the desired outcome.
>
> (Auda, 2021, p. 69)

There are five overlapping and interconnected Maqasid methodology steps: (1) purpose, (2) cycles of reflection, (3) framework, (4) critical studies of literature and reality and (5) formative theories and principles. Figure 6.1 depicts the five stages of the Maqasid methodology.

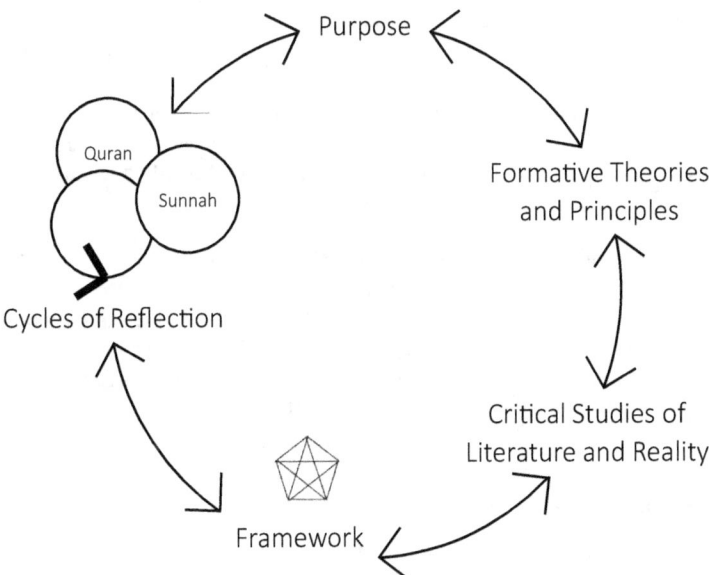

Figure 6.1 Five steps of the Maqasid Methodology
Source: Auda (2021). With kind permission.

76 Islāmic scholarship in research

The five stages of the Maqasid Methodology is a cyclical process but also do not constitute a rigid process that must be followed in sequence. The application of the stages and their entry point would be dependable upon the research question, the competence of the researcher and the available resources. When thinking of applying the Maqasid Methodology in Islāmic psychology, it is worthwhile valuable to reflect on the Higher Objectives of Islāmic Law (*Maqasid Ash-Shar'iah*): the preservation of the religion; the preservation of the self/soul; the preservation of lineage/offspring, progeny, honour; the preservation of the mind/intellect ('*aql*); and the preservation of the wealth. At this point, one could potentially assess how different psychological theories and perspectives are aligned or are incongruent from these higher objectives, or how the purpose of my research is aligned with the dimensions of the higher objectives.

The first step in any Islāmic activities is to set one's intent (niyyah). Allāh says in the Qur'ān:

فَأَقِمْ وَجْهَكَ لِلدِّينِ حَنِيفًا ۚ فِطْرَتَ ٱللَّهِ ٱلَّتِي فَطَرَ ٱلنَّاسَ عَلَيْهَا ۚ لَا تَبْدِيلَ لِخَلْقِ ٱللَّهِ ۚ ذَٰلِكَ ٱلدِّينُ ٱلْقَيِّمُ وَلَٰكِنَّ أَكْثَرَ ٱلنَّاسِ لَا يَعْلَمُونَ

- So, direct your face [i.e., self] toward the religion, inclining to truth. [Adhere to] the fitrah of God upon which He has created [all] people. No change should there be in the creation of God. That is the correct religion, but most of the people do not know.

(Ar-Rūm 30:30)

The rationale for *niyyah* is reflected in the following: In a *Hadīth*, 'Umar bin Al Khattab reported that the Apostle of Allāh (ﷺ) as saying 'Surely, all actions are but driven by intentions' (Abu Dâwud). According to Zarabozo (2008)

> Imam Abu Dâwud stated that this *Hadīth* is one-half of Islām; that is, Islām comprises what is apparent, the deeds of Islām, as well as what is not apparent, the intention behind the deeds. Al-Shafi'ee also said that it encompasses half of knowledge, meaning that the religion concerns both what is external and what is internal. The deeds are the external aspect and the intention behind them is the internal aspect.

(p. 98)

Purpose

Once an intent is made, the setting of the purpose (*qasd/maqsid*) of the research follows suit. In research activities, worship takes the form of producing beneficial knowledge and introducing a useful contribution to thought and action from an Islāmic perspective. What is the purpose of the research?

Islamic scholarship in research

In conventional research, there is usually the statement of the problem or problem definition that is identified and examined, whereas in the Maqasid Methodology it is the definition of purpose (Purpose definition) that is being examined. Auda (2021) clearly distinguishes between these problem definition and purpose definition, stating

> the maqasid methodology in conformance with revelation is purpose-, not problem-, oriented. And while a certain perception of problems could be redefined through purposes, purposes should not be redefined through a certain perception of problems.
>
> (p. 111)

The other question that needs further reflection is 'Why am I carrying out this research?' The research process becomes purpose-driven, having been identified the Revelation or inferred from it, and enables the researcher to have a constructive alignment with divine objectives in the achievement of the purpose.

Cycles of reflection

The cycles of reflection of the Qur'ān-linking with the *Sunnah* is the second stage in the Maqasid Methodology. It is dynamic in nature is a continuous process throughout the enquiry or research. This stage is

> The one indispensable feature of the methodology that cannot be replaced or compromised is the Cycles of Reflection (*dawraat al-tadabbur*) upon the Qur'ân and *Sunnah*. This is the Maqasid Methodology's very core step that no scholar or researcher in Islāmic Studies [or in other disciplines] can do without."
>
> (Auda, 2021, p. 102)

Figure 6.2 depicts the cycles of reflections. Once the researcher has defined their research purpose, they reflect on the appropriate and relevant verses of the Qur'ān and *Sunnah* for specific positioning and guidance. There will be several reflective activities, forming part of the cycles of reflections; that the researcher will undertake in order to arrive at the clarity of the research purpose. Auda (2021) highlighted that the '[a]t this stage of the research, the researcher is not at liberty to be selective in their study of certain verses, Hadīths, dimensions, themes and techniques, but must instead perform full Cycles of Reflections' (p. 114).

أَفَلَا يَتَدَبَّرُونَ ٱلْقُرْءَانَ أَمْ عَلَىٰ قُلُوبٍ أَقْفَالُهَآ

- Then do they not reflect upon the *Qur'ān* [(*yatadabbarun*), or are there locks upon [their] hearts?

(Muhammad 47:24).

78 *Islāmic scholarship in research*

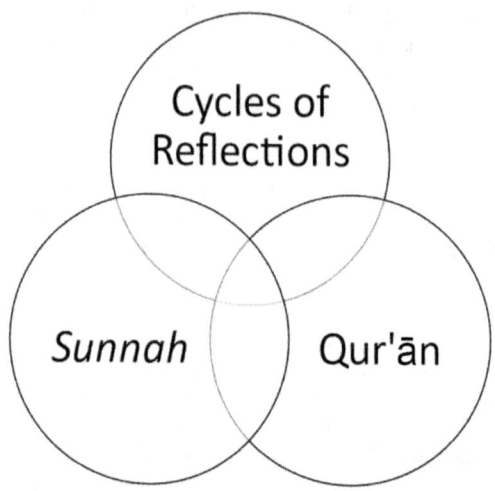

Figure 6.2 Cycles of reflections

In the exegesis of Ibn Kathir (2000), '(Will they not then reflect upon the Qur'ân, or are there locks upon their hearts) means, there indeed are locks upon some hearts, firmly closing them so that none of its meanings can reach them.' Reflecting on the Qur'ân is an exercise in the search for guidance and a cure for the spiritual diseases of the heart (*qalb*). Beside the use of regular introspection using the cycles of reflections on the Qur'ân and *Sunnah*, it also provide a focus on the research's methodological objectives. The search should focus on seeking out basic meanings/elements or themes based on the Qur'ānic worldview and the outcomes would lead to the composite Maqasid framework. A mind map is a useful tool to identify the web of meanings of the research theme.

Framework

There are seven elements in the framework that conceptualise an Islāmic worldview composite: concepts (*mafahim*), objectives (*maqasid*), values (*qiyam*), commands (*awamir*), universal laws (*sunan*), groups (*fi'at*), and proofs (*hujaj*). This framework is presented in Figure 6.3.

However, as Auda (2021) pointed out that

> While definitive in their presence and meaning, each of the Seven Elements is open to further refinement, exploration and additions. Each element presents webs of meanings with cores and clusters that intersect,

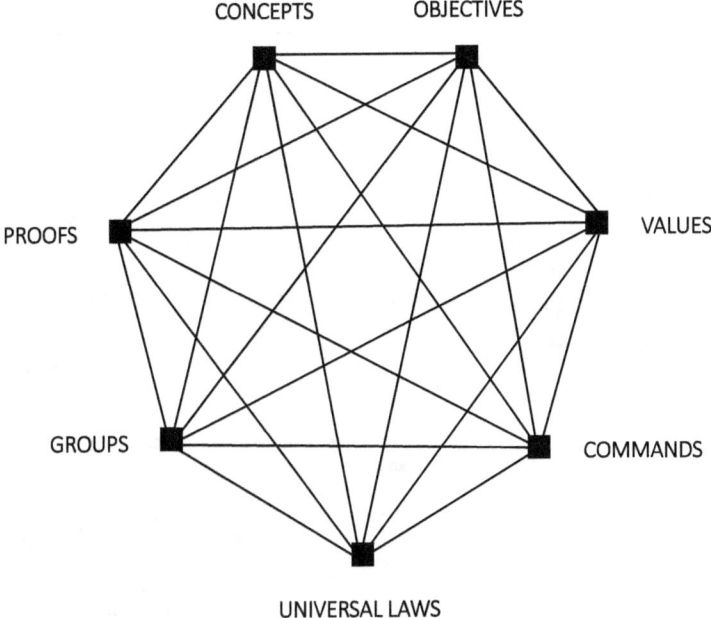

Figure 6.3 The seven elements of the Maqasid framework
Source: Auda (2021). With kind permission.

overlap and integrate seamlessly into one another. This is due to the purposely designed and hence coherent nature of Revelation. Accordingly, these elements are not mutually exclusive categories.

(p. 151)

Table 6.2 provides an overview of the seven-element perceptualisation of the framework. It is important to note that the basic guideline for contemplating all these seven elements is that 'they are to be understood through their textual expressions (*nass*) and through inference (*istinbat*) from their linguistic and webbed manifestations in the revelation' (Auda, 2021, p. 152).

Critical studies of literature and reality

This is the fourth stage in the Maqasid Methodology and critical dialogues/ studies emerged a source of enquiry and consolidation of *'ilm* (knowledge). This is a form of the critical review of the literature from both classical and modern literature from Islāmic and non-Islāmic sources, due to the latter not

Table 6.2 Seven-element perceptualisation of the framework

Elements	Arabic	Characteristics
Concepts	Mafahim	Key words with authority and meaning. Focus on core issues on Qur'ān and *Sunnah*. Correct deviations in understanding the web of meanings.
Objectives	Maqasid	Intention and purposes understood from the Qur'ān and *Sunnah*. Based on realised in the lived reality.
Values	Qiyam	Positive and negative. Denote the importance that humans must place on thoughts, actions and all created matter.
Commands	Awamir	Positive and negative. Orders that govern human behaviour in the Qur'ān and *Sunnah*. Clarify what is beneficial and reprehensible.
Universal laws	Sunan	Laws of creation, natural and social based on the Qur'ān and *Sunnah*. Govern human actions. Promote awareness in human thought and action.
Groups	Fi'at	Parties, human and otherwise identified in the Qur'ān and *Sunnah*. Members and characteristics are detailed. Special reference to human categories, both positive and negative, in order to increase awareness.
Proofs	Hujaj	Aim is to establish truths in the minds and hearts of the believer. Signs (*ayat*) and guideposts (*alamat*). Reinforcing the truth of arguments (*burhan*). Or the soundness of logic (*mantiq*).

Source: Adapted from the text Auda (2021).

being outsourced from an Islāmic worldview or methodology. Auda (2021) argued that

> The Islāmic perspective (*manzur/muntalaq*) represented by the fundamental premises of the Maqasid Methodology differ in fundamental ways from other philosophies and ideologies, despite an acknowledgement of possible overlaps and similarities in many values, ideas and applications.
>
> (p. 127)

It is also a challenging thought of not categorising knowledge as Islāmic and on non-Islāmic source. Thus, all knowledge from comes from Allāh, The Almighty. It is important to note that while identifying and drawing on non-Islāmic source of knowledge, this knowledge should be congruent with Islāmic beliefs and practices and does not 'betray the fundamental tenets of Islām and the core teachings of Revelation' (Auda, 2021, p. 11).

Islāmic scholarship in research 81

A critical analysis of the literature would enable the researcher to gain a wider perspective of the theme of the research this enabling the refinement a topic and frame research questions. It is good practice to summarise and analyse previous research and theories; identify areas of controversy and contested claims; and highlight any gaps that may exist in research to date. There is also the critical engagement with lived realities. This means to have a critical assessment of lived realities based on the Islāmic or Qur'ānic worldview. Auda (2021) suggested that

> To perform this critical assessment of the reality, a comparison should be carried out between two frameworks, fully or partially. One is the Islāmic framework that the *mujtahid* [scholar] developed based on the purposes and Cycles of Reflection, and the other is a similar framework that contains the main elements that describe the lived reality. Describing the reality involves describing communities, organisations, professions, states, laws, technologies, natural environment, animals, organisms, etc.
> (p. 133)

Formative theories and principles

The final stage is the development of formative theories and principles based on the comprehensive information that the composite frameworks (concepts, objectives, values, commands, universal laws, groups, and proofs) generate. This complex stage demand specific skills and Islāmic scholarship. The intellectual discourse operated during this process is not based on inductive method of reasoning but on 'the Quranic expression of emergence as the concepts of "*tawallud*" or "*nushu*" (Qur'ān 2:333, 3:47, 11:72, 71:27, 112:3 and 6:98, 13:12, 23:14, 24:55, 6:73, respectively)'(Auda, 2021, p. 138). Auda (2021) has suggested that

> The conclusion of theories and principles from the webs of meaning and critical studies of the literature and lived reality, also differ from the traditional – and typical – process of induction. Induction involves the search for instances in the texts where a certain meaning manifests.
> (pp. 137–138)

However, to fully understand the Maqasid Methodology, there is a need to have a good understanding and comprehension of the seven elements of the Maqasid Framework.

Conclusion

This chapter presented the basic steps of the Maqasid Methodology, namely, purpose, cycles of reflections, critical studies of literature and reality, framework and formative theories and principles. Auda (2021) suggested that '[a]ll of the proposed five methodological steps, from defining a purpose to concluding theories and principles, would benefit from the above methods of reading the Qur'ân and integrating its meanings' (p. 137). In order to apply the Maqasid Methodology to research in Islāmic psychology would require further refinement of the Methodology accompanied with cycles of reflections. In the context of research in Islāmic psychology

> [a]ll sciences are based on frameworks of concepts, objectives, values, commands, universal laws, groups and proofs, and thinking that any of these elements 'has nothing to do with faith' is not sanctioned by Revelation.
> (Auda, 2021, pp. 128–129)

However, Islāmic psychologists and psychotherapists are expected to reorient psychology in accordance with the Qur'ānic worldview, which is drawn through a composite framework of cycles of reflection on divine revelation. This methodology is a comprehensive framework for understanding and applying Islāmic sources of knowledge in a unique interdisciplinary context. One of the main challenges facing Islāmic psychology is knowledge integration of Islāmic ethics and studies with secular psychology. What is lacking is a common methodology or conceptual framework that can integrate Islāmic epistemologies and ontologies and secular sources of knowledge. This book makes an attempt to remedy this situation. In conclusion, 'Re-envisioning Islāmic Scholarship' challenges the traditional approach to research and emphasises on the broader need for a more relevant and holistic approach in the quest for the development of Islāmic scholarship in contemporary society. Above all, the researchers in Islāmic psychology and psychotherapy needs to develop familiarity with the Maqasid Methodology and identify those dimensions that relate most closely to purpose of the research.

References

Abu Dâwud. *Sunan Abi Dâwud Dawud 2201.* In-book reference: Book 13, Hadith 27. English translation: Book 12, Hadith 2195. Sahih (Al-Albani).

Auda, J. (2021). *Re-envisioning Islāmic Scholarship: Maqasid Methodology as a New Approach.* Swansea: Claritas Publishing House.

Auda, J. (2022). Journal of Contemporary Maqasid Studies (JCMS): Methodological aspirations. *Journal of Contemporary Maqasid Studies,* 1(1), i–iv. https://doi.org/10.52100/jcms.v1i1.60.

Ibn Kathir. (2000). *Tafsir Ibn Kathir* (J. Abualrub, N. Khitab, H. Khitab, A. Walker, M. Al-Jibali, & S. Ayoub, Trans.). Saudi Arabia: Darussalam Publishers and Distributors.

Najimudeen, M. R. (n.d.). Re-envisioning Islāmic scholarship: Maqasid methodology as a new approach. *ICR Journal*, 13(1), 168–171. https://doi.org/10.52282/ICR.V13I1.906.

Zarabozo, Jamaal al-Din M. (2008). *Commentary on the Forty Hadith of al-Nawawi*. Denver, CO: Al-Basheer Company for Publication and Translation.

7 Research proposal

Applying the Maqasid Methodology

Introduction

This is a tentative attempt on the development of a research proposal based on the Maqasid methodology (Auda, 2021). The research proposal is titled 'Predictors of Role Legitimacy, Role Adequacy and Role Support of University Lecturers in knowledge integration of Islāmic Studies and Ethics in the Psychology Curriculum.'[1] The research proposal will make use of the five overlapping and interconnected Maqasid Methodology steps: (1) Purpose, (2) cycles of reflection, (3) framework, (4) critical studies of literature and reality and (5) formative theories and principles (see Figure 7.1). The rationale for using this approach is based on the notion that it provides a holistic framework for seeking revelational guidance by performing continuous cycles of reflections during the research process. Before delving in the purpose (*qasd*) of this research, the intent (*niyyah*) is undertaken. The issue of intention has been examined in Chapter 6.

Purpose of research

In Islāmic psychology, the broad focus of the research is to guide man to divine revelation and teachings of Islām and embrace the presence of Allāh, the Almighty, taking into account the components of the *Maqasid al-Shari'ah* (the Higher Objectives of Islāmic law). It has been suggested that

> [t]he sense of direction of any research and indeed the entire domain, provided by the Qur'ān centered on guiding the individuals how to earn Allāh's grace and bliss in this world and in hereafter, by encouraging them to doing that which pleases Allāh the Exalted. The intent as well as the broad focus of the research therefore is to guide man to divine teachings of Islām, bringing him out of darkness of disbelief, perversion, injustice, wrong-doing, ignorance into the light of belief, justice, knowledge and social harmony.
>
> (Auda, 2021, p. 148)

DOI: 10.4324/9781003346241-7

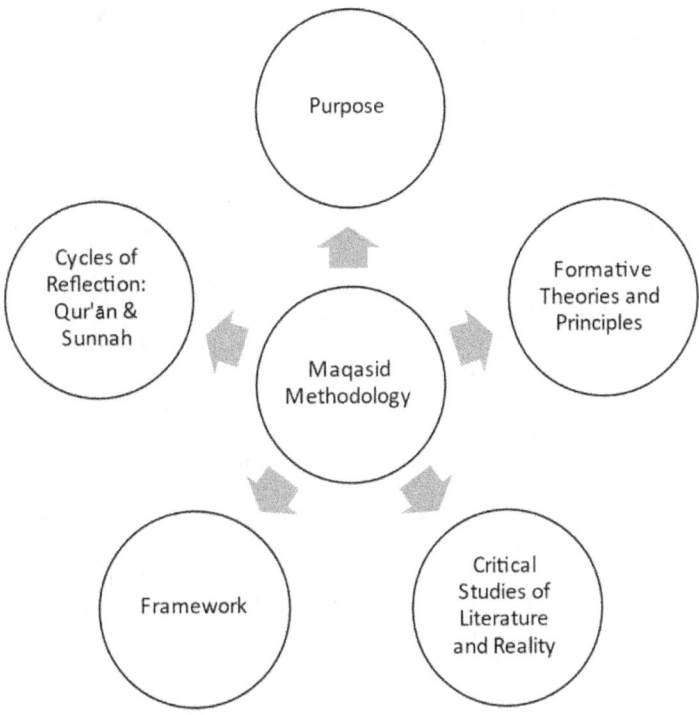

Figure 7.1 The Maqasid Methodology

Hence, Allāh says in the Qur'ān:

كِتَٰبٌ أَنزَلْنَٰهُ إِلَيْكَ لِتُخْرِجَ ٱلنَّاسَ مِنَ ٱلظُّلُمَٰتِ إِلَى ٱلنُّورِ بِإِذْنِ رَبِّهِمْ إِلَىٰ صِرَٰطِ ٱلْعَزِيزِ ٱلْحَمِيدِ

- *We have revealed to you, [O Muhammad], that you might bring mankind out of darknesses into the light by permission of their Lord – to the path of the Exalted in Might, the Praiseworthy.*

(Ibrāheem 14:1)

In the context of the present research, the purpose is about the preservation of faith and the preservation of intellect (*'akl*). This preservation of the Islāmic faith and intellect paves the way for knowledge integration of the Islāmic ethics and psychology in psychology knowledge. As Auda (2021) stated '[w]orship is not only expressed in the performance of Islāmic rituals but is also expressed in every thought and act that one undertakes with the genuine intention of heedfulness (*taqwa*)' (p. 111). The purpose of the study is to examine the role of moral values, role legitimacy, role adequacy and role support of university lecturers in knowledge integration in the psychology curriculum.

Cycles of reflections – Framework

In the cycles of reflections' stage of the Maqasid Methodology, the focus is on searching for basic meanings or components that articulate the Islāmic worldview. Due to the limitations of the nature and scope of the proposal, it would not be possible to provide a comprehensive mind map based on the cycles of reflections. However, the contents of a preliminary survey of the cycles of reflections upon the Qur'ān and the *Sunnah* while researching the basic elements linked to concepts of role, role behaviour and role model (*Oswah*) onto a Vertical Chevron List is presented in Figure 7.2, which represents the Seven Element Framework: Concepts, Objectives, Values, Commands, Universal Laws, Groups and Proofs and shows sequential steps in the Framework to emphasise direction.

The Cycles of Reflection (Figure 7.2) of the Qur'ān and the *Sunnah* generate the concept of role model (*oswah*) meaning 'example, and a leader to be followed' for the research proposal. The word *oswah* 'has been mentioned three times in the Qur'ān, twice about Prophet Ibrahim (AS) in verses 4 and 6 of the chapter Al-Mutma'innah (60:4,6).' The Messenger of God, Prophet

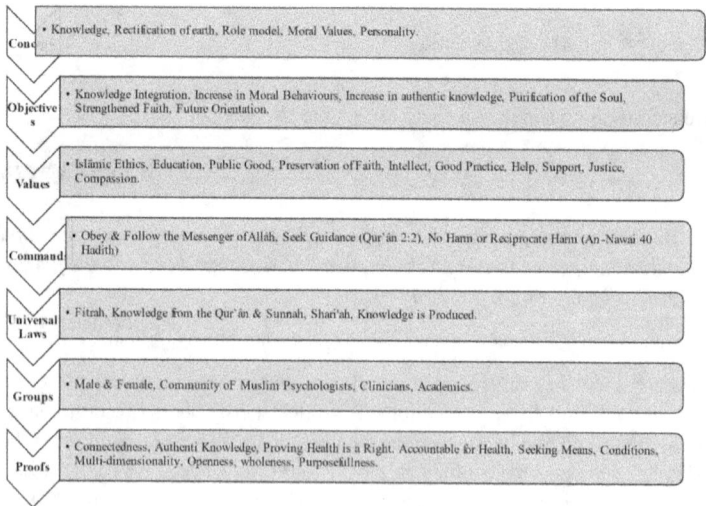

Figure 7.2 Mapping of framework

Muhammad (ﷺ) is mentioned in the above verse, and in verse 21 of the chapter Al-Aḥzāb (33:21), Allāh said in the Qur'ān

لَّقَدْ كَانَ لَكُمْ فِى رَسُولِ ٱللَّهِ أُسْوَةٌ حَسَنَةٌ لِّمَن كَانَ يَرْجُواْ ٱللَّهَ وَٱلْيَوْمَ ٱلْءَاخِرَ وَذَكَرَ ٱللَّهَ كَثِيرًا

- *There has certainly been for you in the Messenger of God an excellent pattern [An example to be followed] for anyone whose hope is in God and the Last Day and [who] remembers God often.*

(Al-Aḥzāb 33:21)

According to exegesis of Ibn Kathir (2000), this verse

is an important principle, to follow the Messenger of Allāh in all his words, and deeds, etc. Hence Allāh commanded the people to take the Prophet as an example on the day of Al-Aḥzāb, with regard to patience, guarding, striving and waiting for Allāh to provide the way out; may the peace and blessings of Allāh be upon him forever, until the Day of Judgement.

This means that the Messenger of Allāh is an excellent role (ﷺ) model as an example and a leader to be followed. Role model is not only about demonstrating the best behaviour but also about demonstrating how to learn from mistakes and failures. There is another concept that is related to moral behaviour, that is, the rectification of earth which is an objection for human nature and in the process and output of knowledge production. Another concept derived from the cycles of reflections is knowledge ('*ilm*) or knowledge production.

In Islām, the meaning of knowledge ('*ilm*) is broader than the notion of the acquisition of knowledge from a Western perspective. Knowledge from an Islāmic perspective is an all-encompassing term focused on theory, action and education embedded with moral and sociopolitical implications. The high significance accorded to knowledge is reflected in 'the nature, virtue, and function of the three related aspects of knowing: possession of knowledge ('*ilm*), dissemination of knowledge, through teaching, education, and moral upbringing (*taʿlīm*), and acquisition of knowledge, through learning, training, and making (*tuʿallum*)' (Akkach, 2019, p. vi). Rosenthal (1970) has provided several meaning of '*ilm* from an Islāmic perspective including *Iḥsās* (sensation, perception); *Idrak* (cognition); *Tadhakkur* (recollection); *Fahm* (understanding); *Fiqh* (comprehension); *Dirayah* (cognisance); *Yaqin* (certainty); *Dhihn* (mind, intellect); *Fikr* (mental process, thinking); *Ra'yi* (opinion); *Istibṣār* (reflection); *Iḥāṭah* (thorough grasp); and *Ẓann* (conjecture).

These connotations of knowledge have implications for the Islāmic research paradigm and the role of the concept of *fiqh*, as one of the most central concepts in Islām. According to the revelation '*fiqh* is: (1) a deep understanding of Islām as a *din*, i.e., way of life and a worldview, (2) a deep understanding of the proofs/signs (ayat) of Allāh, (3) a high capacity for sound judgement and leadership, and (4) the ability to teach knowledge and (5) realise knowledge for the benefit of Muslims and humanity in this life and the next.

(Auda, 2021, p. 15)

Fiqh and knowledge are bound together and cannot be examined in isolation. In this context, psychology or social sciences should not be viewed as separate realms from the study of the branch of knowledge of *fiqh* (*'ilm*) in the broader sense. There is some misconception about the terminology of *fiqh* because it is assumed to be related only to the 'law.' However, it is argued that

> *fiqh* was a deep understanding in every branch of knowledge (*'ilm*) that Muslims developed, *fuqaha* [scholars] were the experts in these branches. The *fuqaha* who studied law, politics, sociology, medicine, biology, chemistry, mathematics, astronomy, optics, architecture, urban planning, etc., did not make a separation between their sciences and the concepts of "*'ilm*" or "*fiqh*" and they considered their books to be reflection upon the ayat [verse] of Allah in the horizons and the souls.

(Auda, 2021, pp. 16–17)

All this leads us to maintain that the Islāmic research paradigm is bind to the fundamental belief that knowledge is integrated, connected with the Creator and wholistic rather than 'an individual entity . . . may be owed by an individual' (Wilson, 2001, p. 176). Besides, divine revelation is also the main source of knowledge. Malkawi (2014) suggested that the classical Muslim scholars, despite their different schools of thought, agreed that

> knowledge should be interconnected, complementary, and organically linked to the knowledge of God. In the view of these scholars, the fact that all sciences originate from a single divine source is the foundation for the ultimate integration and unity of knowledge.

(p. 12)

This integration of knowledge, especially the revealed and the created knowledge, is a necessity that will bring balance to the understanding of reality and truth.

Conduct critical studies of literature and reality

The fourth step is to conduct critical studies of literature and reality. A brief overview is provided here. In this phase, there is the utilisation of knowledge from the so-called non-Islāmic sources that are not incongruent with Islāmic beliefs and practices and are relevant to the nature of humans. Auda (2021) maintained that

> there may be full utilisation of non-Islāmic ideas and their practical results or tools if these conform to known Islāmic truths, or if they represent a description of the reality that the researcher is studying based on true measures.
>
> (p. 128)

Much of the literature on religion, spirituality and therapy comes from the United States (e.g., Aten & Leach, 2009; Miller, 1999). Hence, some of the recommendations offered may not transfer readily to an Islāmic context and are applicable to the religious landscape of Muslims. However, professional and scientific psychology appears to have rediscovered spirituality and religion during recent years with a large number of literature and publications in major professional journals on spirituality and psychology integration. However, most of professional and scientific psychology during the past century has been antagonistic to issues related to spirituality and religion. Collins (1977) states: '. . . psychology has never shown much interest in religion . . . apart from a few classic studies . . . the topic of religious behaviour has been largely ignored by psychological writers' (p. 95). However, psychology in the twentieth century prided itself on being a robust science and adopting the positivistic Western scientific paradigm in both research and clinical practice. In recent years, the integration of spirituality, and religion in psychology and psychiatry has been legitimised and has received significant attentions due to the effects of spirituality on mental health (Anandarajah & Hight, 2001; Ho & Ho, 2007; Jones et al., 2019; Koenig et al., 2011; Rosmarin, 2018). Spirituality has been recognised as an important feature of the therapeutic process, and it has been suggested that 'religion and spirituality may support the process of counselling by infusing both the client and the therapist with a set of values and principles that strengthen their relationship and improve the therapeutic process' (Frunza et al., 2019, p. 60). Despite the recent rapprochement of psychology and spirituality, and that research and practice both now support benefit of the integration of psychology and religion, some critics have cautioned that the integration of religion and spirituality into psychology is ethically, professionally and scientifically dangerous (Sloan et al., 1999, 2001). In effect, the exclusion of spirituality or religion in the contents of the psychology curriculum and clinical practice has significant implications in meeting the spiritual dimension of the wholistic needs of clients.

A number of constructs need to be examined in this review in order to provide the scope and context of the study. The constructs include knowledge integration, perception of knowledge integration, role legitimacy, role adequacy and role support. Since the late twentieth century, 'knowledge integration' and integrated research have been used in contemporary

Islāmic philosophy to reconcile Islām and modernity and to integrate Islāmic ethics and epistemological values in social sciences. Knowledge integration refers to 'the process of merging two or more originally unrelated knowledge structures into a single structure' (Schneider, 2012). However, from an Islāmic perspective, knowledge integration according to Kasule (2015) "involves integrating Islāmic moral and epistemological values in the various disciplines of knowledge that are taught." (p. 124). Thus, the essence of integrating knowledge, from an Islāmic perspective, is to bring knowledge from the different compartments and sources under one umbrella to achieve a given goal or a set of objectives. Knowledge integration focuses on the integration of empirical evidence (*Ilm 'aqli*) with revealed knowledge (*Ilm 'naqli*), and the synthesis of both sources of knowledge into an integrated model based on *Tawhîdic* paradigm. This means that knowledge integration is based on reconstructing the epistemology, in the context of psychology, based on the Islāmic worldview. As AbuSulyman (1993) stated:

> The process of bringing the religious and the secular elements together is, from the Islāmic point of view, a restoration of the link between reason and revelation, or between the role of the mind in appreciating (comprehending and interpreting) revelation and guiding the mind by means of the revelation's objectives, its comprehensive and universal outlook, and its living and civilization values. Thus, the joining of the two wings in the pursuit of reform in an intellectual process in its methodology and style.
>
> (p. 21).

Due to limited literature on the factors influencing the integration of Islāmic psychology and ethical values in the psychology curriculum in higher education, there is a need to conclude from other literature and research evidence. For example, several factors influencing the integration of technology integration into the learning and teaching process in higher education have been identified. Schiler (2003) identified a number of variables that can have a significant influence on the adoption of technology. These include educational level, age, gender, educational experience, experience with the computer and attitude towards computers. There is also evidence to suggest that successful implementation of technology integration, attitudes and teacher-related variables are the most powerful predictors of integration (Avidov-Ungar & Eshet-Alkakay, 2011; Becker, 2000). However, if teachers' perceptions are negative, this would result in a lack of integration of technology (Hutchison & Reinking, 2011). Both the Theory of Planned Behaviour and Roger's Diffusion of Innovation emphasised on the importance of perception and knowledge attitudes in the implementation of any new or different practice (Ajzen, 1991; Holt et al., 2010).

The call for the Islāmisation of psychology knowledge, now replaced by knowledge integration (Badri, 2018) (Rassool, 2020, 2021a, 2021b, 2022), reinforces the requirements for psychology university lecturers to prioritise the need to prepare their students in Islāmic psychology. Knowledge integration is an important tool in the deconstruction of Eurocentric and secular psychology knowledge. For university lecturers to engage fully with knowledge integration of Islāmic studies and ethics in the psychology curriculum, it needs clarity over the roles they should fulfil along with their competence. Given the wholistic and ecological framework underpinning Islāmic spirituality in Islāmic psychology, psychology university lecturers are well placed to decolonise secular psychology and integrate Islāmic studies and ethics in the psychology curriculum. The roles of university psychology lectures focus on the production of psychology, teaching and research. The following key roles are the starting point for psychology university lecturers in relation to introducing Islāmic spirituality and ethics in the psychology curriculum.

- To engage with the theme of Islāmic spirituality and ethics as part of their educational and teaching practices.
- To engage with the theme of Islāmic spirituality and ethics as part of their research practices.
- To engage with the theme of Islāmic spirituality and ethics as part of their clinical practices.
- To support colleagues and students in the implementation of knowledge integration in educational, research and clinical settings.

There is limited literature on knowledge integration of Islāmic psychology and Islāmic ethical values in the psychology curriculum. To date, there are only two studies that focus on the implementation of the integration on knowledge of Islām and psychology. In a study by Fahmi (2018) on the implementation of integration of knowledge of Islām and psychology with a sample of 32 lecturers. The findings suggest that though most of the lecturers seemed to lack the capacity to provide any logical explanation of the connection between Islām and psychology. What was interesting about the findings of this study is that none of the psychology lecturers have a background in Islāmic Studies. The findings from a study by Rassool (2023) on the readiness of university lecturers on knowledge integration of Islāmic ethics and Islāmic psychology in the psychology curriculum showed that the majority of the lecturers had high Islāmic moral values, were highly motivated to learn, and had significantly positive attitude towards knowledge integration of Islāmic ethics and Islāmic psychology. The psychology lecturers were also found to be making limited contributions to knowledge integration and paid restricted attention to the recent developments in the field. However, the majority of lecturers were found to experience a high level of role legitimacy (refers to the belief that whether they have a legitimate right to change and modify psychology) and role support, but they also experienced a low level of role adequacy (refers how knowledgeable Muslim psychologists are about Islāmic psychology and Islāmic sciences to implement knowledge integration). The lack of preparation, knowledge, experts, guidance, and resources [books, materials] were identified as the main barriers to the prevention of knowledge integration in teaching practices. The main facilitators identified in enhancing knowledge integration include having more workshops and courses in Islāmic psychology and psychotherapy. One interesting finding described by a participant is having knowledge in both Islāmic studies and psychology would enable knowledge integration in teaching practices.

One of the constructs of this study is the perception of knowledge integration. There is a relationship between perception and worldview and the latter is regarded as a personal perception of their relationship with the world. Perception questions differ from other types of attitudinal questions as the former is how you view the work from an individual lens. In contrast, an attitude question is the reaction to your perception of their relationship with the world. According to Lavrakas (2008), "Survey questions that assess perception, as opposed to those assessing factual knowledge, are aimed at identifying the processes that (a) underlie how individuals acquire, interpret, organise, and, generally make sense of (i.e. form beliefs about) the environment in which they live; and (b) help measure the extent to which such perceptions affect individual behaviours and attitudes as a function of an individual's past experiences, biological makeup, expectations, goals, and/or culture." Bem's Self-Perception Theory (1972) proposed that people infer their attitudes from their behaviour in contrast to the notion that attitudes determine behaviour. The principle of the self-perception theory states that "Individuals come to "know" their own attitudes, emotions, and other internal states partially by inferring them from observations of their own overt behaviour and/or the circumstances in which this behaviour occurs. Thus, to the extent that internal cues are weak, ambiguous, or uninterpretable, the individual is functionally in the same position as an outside observer, an observer who must necessarily rely upon those same external cues to infer the individual's inner state" (p. 2). Self-perception theory proposes that there is a causal link between behaviour and attitude reversing the sequence of causation from attitude to behaviour. The constructs of perception, values and attitudes have long been known to be predictors of behaviour (Ajzen, 1991; Eagley & Chaiken, 1993; Glasman & Albarracín, 2006).

The constructs of role adequacy (feeling knowledgeable about one's work), role legitimacy (believing that one has the right to address certain issues), and role support have long been key theoretical constructs regarding explanations of why various helping professionals are reluctant to address certain issues in their respective fields and explain the extent of their willingness to take on new dimensions to their professional role (Shaw et al., 1978;

Skinner et al., 2005; Loughran et al., 2010). Research studies have provided evidence that role support was the strongest predictor of role legitimacy and role adequacy was support and the perceived usefulness of education (Skinner et al., 2005). The authors conclude that the identification of support is a key predictor of role adequacy and legitimacy which reinforces the importance of organisational support rather than focusing exclusively on the knowledge, skills and experience of an individual worker. Shaw et al. (1978) suggested that anxieties about role adequacy are related to worker's feelings about their lack of required knowledge and skills, and uncertainty about their professional boundaries to recognise and respond positively in an effective manner. Another aspect of Shaw et al.'s (1978) study is related to the worker's belief that they were not being supported and thus received no assistance in terms of advice, support and consultation about the most effective option in their total engagement. Shaw et al. (1978) maintained that role adequacy, role legitimacy and lack of role support are interconnected in a complex relationship and workers who exhibit these factors are described as having role insecurity. It has been suggested that "[l]egitimacy is an internal value that is linked to personal feelings of obligation and responsibility to others. In these ways, it is similar to the moral values that are also an internal motivational guide to behaviour" (Tyler, 2006, p. 390). In this context, role legitimacy and moral values are internalised and interconnected and there is a strong possibility that both concepts may influence each other. That is integrating knowledge from Islāmic studies and ethics in the psychology curriculum is a legitimate responsibility of university lecturers which is acting in ways consistent with Islāmic personal moral values. Role legitimacy, role adequacy and role support have been ascribed to the label of role behaviours. It is within this background and context that this current study evolves.

The theory of role behaviours (role adequacy, role legitimacy and role support) is being used to understand the barriers and enhancement of knowledge integration of Islāmic studies and ethics in the psychology curriculum. This theory points to qualities of Muslim psychology lecturers as including understanding, accepting and encouraging Islāmic values towards knowledge integration based on their Islāmic moral values. This configuration of role behaviours and values has the ascribed label of "Islāmic Ethical Commitment." Figure 7.3 describes the cycle which links lack of knowledge, low ethical intelligence,[2] to low Islāmic ethical commitment. The cycle could be triggered by an event at any point for instance a lack of understanding of knowledge integration on the part of the psychologists or having low ethical intelligence (Islāmic values) leading to role insecurity, role legitimacy, and role adequacy.

This lack of the "Islāmic Ethical Commitment" may be due to the lack of clarity of their roles and uncertainty as to the relevance of their knowledge and skills- they suffered from role legitimacy, role adequacy and role ambiguity. It is assumed that while Muslim psychologists may be professionally competent in general when it came to teaching general or sub-disciplines of psychology

94 Research proposal

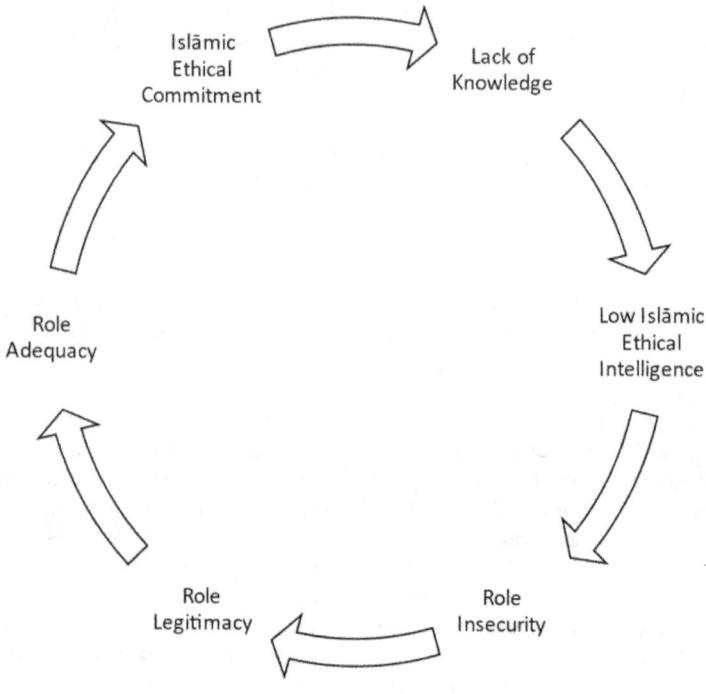

Figure 7.3 The Cycle of Islāmic Ethical Commitment

they often had little or no preparation and consequently, they lacked knowledge and skills in knowledge integration. It may be inferred that psychology lecturers are uncertain about their legitimacy to undertake this extended role and rights to teach Islāmic ethics and studies embedded in the psychology knowledge. It was therefore concluded that bringing about changes in role behaviours would lead to greater knowledge integration effectiveness.

The construct of moral values will be based on the divine revelation of the Qur'ān and Sunnah. This concept consists of four: wisdom (hikmah), courage (*shaja'ah*), temperance ('*iffah*), and justice ('*adl*), (Al-Ghazâlî, cited in Sherif, 1975, p. 29). This is what constitutes the Islāmic moral or ethical concept of *Akhlāq*. Thus, "Islāmic moral basic is based on the principle to attain wisdom, courage, temperance, and justice. These values are categorised as vertical values and related to horizontal values. "The Islāmic moral vertical refers to God-consciousness while the Islāmic moral horizontal refers to social life responsibilities" (Nuriman & Fauzan, 2017, p. 279). However, there has been little research into the moral values, role adequacy, role legitimacy and role support of university lectures in the implementation of knowledge

Research proposal 95

integration in the psychology curriculum. The purpose of the study was to examine the role of moral values, role legitimacy role adequacy and role support of university lecturers in knowledge integration in the psychology curriculum.

Aims, research questions and hypotheses

The study aims to examine the moral values and role behaviours of university lecturers on their readiness for knowledge integration of Islāmic psychology and ethical values in the psychology curriculum. The study was guided by the following research question and hypothesis:

- What are the Islāmic moral values of the university lecturers?
- What is the status of role adequacy, role legitimacy and role support of university lecturers' readiness for knowledge integration of Islāmic psychology and Islāmic ethical values in the psychology curriculum?
- What is the perception of university lectures on knowledge integration?
- To what extent do Islāmic moral values have an influence on the readiness of knowledge integration of Islāmic studies and Islāmic psychology in the psychology curriculum?
- To what extent do role behaviours have an influence on the readiness of knowledge integration of Islāmic studies and Islāmic psychology in the psychology curriculum?
- To what extent do the demographic variables have an influence on moral values, role behaviours and perceptions of knowledge integration?

In addition, while this research is exploratory, it was hypothesised that

- H1: The moral values of university lecturers will be better predictors of the readiness for knowledge integration.
- H2: The role behaviours of university lecturers will be better predictors of the readiness for knowledge integration.
- H3: The combined role behaviours and moral values will be better predictors of knowledge integration of Islāmic ethics and Islāmic psychology in the psychology curriculum.
- H4: Selected demographic variables of the university lecturers will be better predictors of knowledge integration

Formative theories and principles

The final step in the formative theories and principles is the connections and interrelationships of the Maqasid Framework. More cycles of reflections and conceptual or theoretical development are needed to be able to apply the Maqasid Methodology in a wholistic manner. Figure 7.4 shows the conceptual

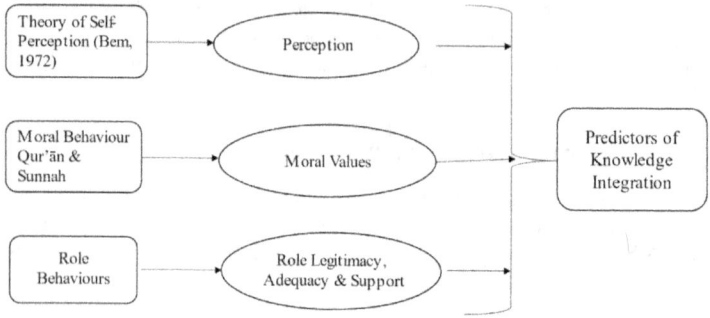

Figure 7.4 The theoretical and conceptual framework

and theoretical models in this study. In this model, a variety of constructs of personal and professional variables are critical in determining the predictors of the readiness of university lecturers to integrate Islāmic psychology and Islāmic ethical values in the psychology curriculum. The study is guided by the self-perception theory (Bem, 1972), and the conceptual framework of role behaviours which form the basis for the study hypotheses and choice of research methodologies.

In the context of this study, role adequacy is defined as having the appropriate knowledge and ethical values to implement knowledge integration and role legitimacy is the extent to which one has the right to address knowledge integration in psychology. Role support is the provision of professional and personal support at individual and organisational levels. The three core constructs of this study are perception, morality and role behaviours (role legitimacy, role adequacy and role support). These constructs interact together and are the prime factors in determining university lecturers' readiness to teach and implement knowledge integration and ethical values in the psychology curriculum.

Methodology

Research design

This is a multi-method research design involving both quantitative and qualitative research methodologies. This integrated or mixed methods research

> involves collecting both quantitative and qualitative data (in response to quantitative and qualitative research questions), the merging, linking, or combining of the two sources of data, and then conducting research as a single study or a longitudinal project with multiple phases.
> (Creswell & Garrett, 2008, p. 326)

In the context of research from an Islāmic perspective, integrated research is the process of synthesising research methodologies and approaches (empirical, rational) with Islāmic studies methodologies. Integrated research focuses on the integration of empirical evidence (*Ilm 'aqli*) with revealed knowledge (*Ilm 'naqli*), and the synthesis of both sources of knowledge into an integrated model based on *Tawhīdic* paradigm. One of the strengths of the integrated research methodology would decrease the limitations of both methodological approaches thus providing important 'converging evidence' of the phenomenon under study.

Sample

The sample for this study would be purposively selected (purposive sampling) faculty members of universities in a number of countries (multi-centre) with Muslim-majority population. The purposeful sampling will be in the form of quota sampling. It has been suggested that

> [q]uota sampling selects fixed or equivalent numbers of subjects from predetermined groups to ensure that the study accounts for important differences between the groups. This requires the researcher to make a priori assumptions about what types of differences between subjects are important, and the researcher then will treat each group of subjects like a separate population pool.
>
> (Kimmons, 2022).

In addition, the author added that '[b]y conducting parallel analyses of groups of subjects, researchers can construct group-based narratives for comparison and ensure that diverse perspectives (in terms of the grouping criterion) are explored in a focused manner.'

Method

Data on the sample were obtained by a self-reported questionnaire, which consisted of four sections: Section A is the demographic data (age, gender, position, academic and professional qualification, duration of teaching experiences). Section B consists of an adaptation of the Sahin Index of Islāmic Moral Values (SIIMV; Francis et al., 2008) which comprises 17 items. It was constructed around the key Muslim ethical concept *akhlāq*, meaning disposition, an individual's fundamental value orientation in life and his/her essential nature of being in the world (Francis et al., 2008). Each item is assessed on a close-ended Likert scale ranging from '1, strongly disagree' to '5, strongly agree.' The Sahin Index of Islāmic Moral Values contains both negative (three items) and positive items (14 items). The negative items were reverse-scored. The original SIIMV has an alpha coefficient of 0.80, which showed that items are consistent and reliable. The adapted Sahin Index of Islāmic Moral Values has an alpha coefficient of 0.77.

Section C is a questionnaire to examine the lecturers' perceptions of knowledge integration. It is an adaptation of the Student Perception of Research Integration Questionnaire (SPRIQ; Visser-Wijnveen et al., 2016) which consists of a 12-item instrument based on three subscales of reflection, participation and motivation. This questionnaire was adapted to form the Lecturer's Perceptions of Knowledge Integration Questionnaire (LPKIQ-12). The LPKIQ-12 consists of three constructs of participation (three items), motivation (four items) and reflection (five items). The construct participation includes items on the involvement of lecturers in knowledge integration and their contributions. The construct reflection includes items focusing on attention being paid to the knowledge integration process leading to implementation. Motivation consists of items concerning an increase in lecturers' enthusiasm and interest in knowledge integration. The items were scored on a 5-point Likert scale, ranging from *very rarely* to *very frequently*. The adapted LPKIQ-12 has an alpha coefficient of 0.90.

Section D consists of a questionnaire measuring the Role Behaviours Questionnaire (RBQ-19) which is an adaptation from the subscales of role adequacy, role legitimacy and role support of the Adolescent Substance Use Problems Perceptions Questionnaire (ASUPPQ; Connors et al., 2019). The adaptations were made by substantially changing the wording to reflect the scope of the study and in some cases new statements were included. There are seven possible responses to each item on a scale of 'strongly agree' to 'strongly disagree.' Low scores denote low level of role behaviours whereas high scores are associated with high level of role behaviours The minimum possible score is 38 and the maximum is 154. The psychometric properties (validity and reliability –Cronbach's alpha) of the RBQ-19 need to be determined.

Statistical analysis

Data analyses will be performed using version 22 of the Statistical Package for the Social Sciences (IBM PASW statistics 22). In addition, descriptive statistics were used to evaluate and analyse the data for the means, medians and standard deviations. Demographic variables will be analysed by using frequency distributions and percentages. For inferential statistics, the study will employ exploratory factor analysis, Pearson's correlation, reliability and multiple linear regressions for data analysis. The multiple regression will be performed to determine the size of the overall relationship between knowledge integration (dependent variable), and perceptions, attitudes and role behaviours (independent variables) and to what extent each of the independent variables contribute to predict readiness for knowledge integration by university lecturers.

Ethical considerations

Ethical approval of the study will be sought from the parent university where the study is being conducted. But approval will also be sought from the universities participating in this research study. General information and a consent form will be provided to participants taking part in the study. All participants will be provided with information regarding their role in the study, the purpose of the study and the data collection methods. Participants will be informed that they have the right to withdraw from the study at any time during any of the procedures. All of the lecturers' interviews and the results of questionnaires with adhere to the proviso of confidentiality and anonymity.

Significance of study

In the context of Islāmisation of knowledge movement and knowledge integration of Islāmic psychology and Islāmic studies in the psychology curriculum, this is a timely study which will provide new insights into the predictors of knowledge integration. Through this research, we would have a better understanding of the process of implementing knowledge integration not only in psychology but also replicated in the social sciences. Our main aim in this study is to address the almost total lack of research evidence on the predictors of role behaviours in knowledge integration in psychology. This study will also add to the current state of knowledge in the field of knowledge integration in psychology and highlights the readiness of university lecturers on the integration of Islāmic psychology and Islāmic ethics in the psychology curriculum. In addition, the findings will identify the role behaviours and the barriers and facilitators that have may have an influence in the implementation of knowledge integration.

Implications of study

The first major practical contribution of the present research is that it provides much-needed empirical data on the role behaviours of university lecturers' readiness for knowledge integration. The findings of the study will have implications at both individual and organisational levels. The findings of the study will nudge Department of Psychology in the universities studied to re-examine their educational and organisational strategies for the implementation of knowledge integration. The findings will provide the Dean of the Faculty of Social Sciences and Heads of Departments of Psychology with information on how to implement and improve the process of knowledge integration. At the individual level, the findings of the study have implications for educators' teaching-learning and evaluating strategies in enhancing knowledge, skills and attitude in knowledge integration. An important implication of the study will point to a specific set of individual moral values that may enhance the readiness of university lecturers towards knowledge integration and the identification of potential barriers and potential facilitators that may support foster or hamper the implementation of knowledge integration. In addition to this, the overview presented in this research will push for new paradigms which will be useful for future discussion and implementation of knowledge integration.

Operational definitions

- Islāmisation: It is 'synonymous, with the term Islamic Revivalism (Renaissance) which is defined as a reform-oriented movement driven by a conscious change in Muslim thought, attitude and behaviour and characterized by a commitment to revive Islamic Civilization' (Al-Tamim, n.d., p. 6).
- Islāmisation of Knowledge:

    Islamization of knowledge is the comprehensive, normative framework for individuals and society, for thought and action, for education and practice, for knowledge and organization, for the rulers and the ruled, for this world and for the world to come. By applying "Islāmization" to everything one does, a Muslim seeks the pleasure of Allāh by practicing what is true and just, through transformation and improvement, to achieve happiness, peace and security in this life as well as in the hereafter.

    (International Institute of Islamic Thought, 1989, p. 84).

- Islāmic psychology: The study of the science of soul, mental processes and behaviour according to the principles of empirical psychology, rationality and divine revelation from the Qur'ān and Sunnah (Rassool, 2020, 2023).
- Knowledge integration: Knowledge integration 'involves integrating Islāmic moral and epistemological values in the various disciplines of knowledge that are taught' (Kasule, 2015, p. 124).
- Moral values: 'They are those values that a person acquires based on their experience. These norms or modes of behaviour are inherited and transmitted by society to citizens. In addition, they determine how to behave correctly or incorrectly' (Pike, 2023).
- Role behaviours: The combination of role legitimacy, role adequacy and role support.
- Role adequacy: It is defined as having the appropriate knowledge and ethical values to implement knowledge integration.
- Role legitimacy: It is the extent to which one has the right to address knowledge integration in psychology.
- Role support: Professional and personal support at individual and organisational levels.
- Perception: 'The way that someone thinks and feels about a company, product, service, etc.' (Cambridge University Press, 2022).

- Self-perception: 'Self-perception theory describes the process in which people, lacking initial attitudes or emotional responses, develop them by observing their own behaviour and coming to conclusions as to what attitudes must have driven that behaviour' (Bem, 1972).

Notes

1. Research proposal submitted as part of the fulfilment of the requirements of the Advanced Course in Maqasid Methodology conducted by Maqasid Institute, leading to a Post-Graduate Certificate in Maqasid Methodology, March 2023.
2. This concept is coined by Professor Dr Anis Ahmad, Vice-Chancellor, Riphah International University. 'Ethical intelligence' is based on the Islāmic concepts of what is acceptable (*Halal*) and what is unacceptable (*Haram*) and is solely based on the Qur'ān and the *Sunnah*. The lecture on 'Psychology: An Islamic Approach' was delivered at the workshop on 'Islamic Psychology Curriculum Development,' 10 February to 13 February 2020, Riphah International University, QIE Campus, Lahore, Pakistan.

References

AbuSulyman, A. H. (1993). *Crisis in the Muslim Mind*. Herndon, VA: International Institute of Islāmic Thought.

Ajzen, I. (1991). The theory of planned behaviour. *Organizational Behavior and Human Decision Processes*, 50(2), 179–211.

Akkach, S. (2019). *Science, Religion and Art in Islam*. Adelaide: University of Adelaide Press.

Al-Tamim, S. (n.d.). *Islamization of Knowledge: The meaning and Definition*. Retrieved from www.academia.edu/35557718/Islamization_of_Knowledge_The_Case_of_Psychology.

Anandarajah, G., & Hight, E. (2001). Spirituality and medical practice: Using the HOPE questions as a practical tool for spiritual assessment. *American Family Physician*, 63, 81–92.

Aten, J. D., & Leach, M. M. (Eds.). (2009). *Spirituality and the Therapeutic Process: A Comprehensive Resource from Intake to Termination*. Washington, DC: American Psychological Association.

Auda, J. (2021). *Re-envisioning Islāmic Scholarship: Maqasid Methodology as a New Approach*. Swansea: Claritas Publishing House.

Avidov-Ungar, O., & Eshet-Alkakay, Y. (2011). Lecturers in a world of change: Lecturers' knowledge and attitudes towards the implementation of innovative technologies in schools. *Interdisciplinary Journal of e-Learning and Lifelong Learning*, 7, 291–303.

Badri, M. (2018). *The Dilemma of Muslim Psychologists*. Kuala Lumpur: Islamic Book Trust.

Becker, H. J. (2000). Findings from the teaching, learning, and computing survey: Is Larry Cuban right? *Education Policy Analysis Archives*, 8(51). Retrieved from https://eric.ed.gov/?q=%22Becker+Henry+Jay%22&id=EJ622351.

Bem, D. J. (1972). Self-perception theory. *Advances in Experimental Social Psychology*, 6, 1–62.

Cambridge University Press. (2022). Perception. In *Cambridge University Online Dictionary*. Retrieved from http://dictionary.cambridge.org/us/dictionary/american-english/attitude.

Collins, A. (1977). Why cognitive science. *Cognitive Science*, 1(1), 1–2.

Connors, E., McKenzie, M., Robinson, P., Tager, M., Scardamalia, K., Oros, M., & Hoover, S. (2019). Adaptation of the drug and drug problems perception questionnaire to assess healthcare provider attitudes toward adolescent substance use. *Preventive Medicine Reports*, 14, 100852. https://doi.org/10.1016/j.pmedr.2019.100852.

Creswell, J. W., & Garrett, A. L. (2008). The "movement" of mixed methods research and the role of educators. *South African Journal of Education*, 28(3), 321–333.

Dalhat, Y. (2015). Introduction to research methodology in Islamic studies. *Journal of Islamic Studies and Culture*, 3(2), 147–152.

Eagley, A. H., & Chaiken, S. (1993). *The Psychology of Attitudes*. San Diego, CA: Harcourt, Brace and Jovanovich.

Fahmi, R. (2018). The implementation of integration on knowledge: Islām-psychology. *Research Journal of Politics, Economics and Management*, 6(1), 63–67.

Francis, L. J., Şahin, A., & Failakawi, F. (2008). Psychometric properties of two Islamic measures among young adults in Kuwait: The Sahin-Francis scale of attitude toward Islam and the Sahin index of Islamic moral values. *Journal of Muslim Mental Health*, 3(1), 9–24.

Frunza, M., Ovidiu, G., & Sandu, F. (2019). The role of spirituality in therapeutic practices. *Journal for the Study of Religions and Ideologies*, 18(53), 60–74.

Glasman, L. R., & Albarracín, D. (2006). Forming attitudes that predict future behavior: A meta-analysis of the attitude-behavior relation. *Psychological Bulletin*, 132(5), 778–822. https://doi.org/10.1037/0033-2909.132.5.778.

Ho, D. Y. F., & Ho, R. T. H. (2007). Measuring spirituality and spiritual emptiness: Toward ecumenicity and transcultural applicability. *Review of General Psychology*, 11(1), 62–74. https://doi.org/10.1037/1089-2680.11.1.62.

Holt, D. T., Helfrich, C. D., Halland, C., & Weiner, B. J. (2010). Are you ready? How health professionals can comprehensively conceptualize readiness for change. *Journal of General Internal Medicine*, 25(1), 50–55.

Hutchison, A., & Reinking, D. (2011). Teachers' perceptions of integrating information and communication technologies into literacy instruction: A national survey in the U.S. *Reading Research Quarterly*, 46(4), 308–329.

International Institute of Islamic Thought. (1989). *Islamization of Knowledge: General Principles and Work Plan*. Herndon, VA: The International Institute of Islamic Thought.

Jones, S., Sutton, K., & Isaacs, A. (2019). Concepts, practices and advantages of spirituality among people with a chronic mental illness in Melbourne. *Journal of Religion & Health*, 58(1), 343–355.

Kasule, O. H. (2015). Integration of knowledge (IOK) and textbook writing for Islāmic universities. *International Journal of Islāmic Thoughts*, 4(1), 123–126.

Kimmons, R. (2022). Sampling: How should I choose a sample for my study? In R. Kimmons (Ed.), *Education Research*. EdTech Books. Retrieved from https://edtechbooks.org/education_research/sampling.

Koenig, H., McCullough M., & Larson D. (2011). *Handbook of Religion and Health*. Oxford: Oxford University Press.

Lavrakas, P. J. (2008). *Encyclopedia of Survey Research Methods* (Vols. 1). Thousand Oaks, CA: Sage Publications.

Loughran, H., Hohman, M., & Finnegan, D. (2010). Predictors of role legitimacy and role adequacy of social workers working with substance-using clients. *The British Journal of Social Work*, 40(1). https://doi.org/10.1093/bjsw/bcn106.

Malkawi, F. H. (2014). *Epistemological Integration: Essentials of an Islāmic Methodology*. Translated from the Arabic by Nancy Roberts. Herndon, VA: International Institute of Islāmic Thought.

Miller, W. R. (Ed.). (1999). *Integrating Spirituality into Treatment: Resources for Practitioners*. Washington, DC: American Psychological Association.

Nuriman, A., & Fauzan, S. (2017). The influence of Islamic moral values on the students' behavior in Aceh. *Dinamika Ilmu*, 17(2), 275–290.

Pike, J. (2023). *Moral Values: What is it, definition and concept*. Retrieved https://crgsoft.com/moral-values/.

Rassool, G. H. (2020). Cognitive restructuring of psychology: The case for a vertical and horizontal integrated, embedded curriculum model for Islāmic psychology. *Islāmic Studies*, 59(4), 477–494.

Rassool, G. H. (2021a). *Islamic Psychology: Human Behaviour and Experience from an Islamic Perspective*. Oxford: Routledge.

Rassool, G. H. (2021b). Decolonising psychology and its (dis) contents. In G. H. Rassool (Ed.), *Islāmic Psychology: Human Behaviour and Experiences from an Islāmic Perspective* (pp. 583–601). Oxford: Routledge.

Rassool, G. H. (2022). Foundation of Islāmic psychology: The 'Dodo Bird' revival, Chapter 1. In G. H. Rassool & M. Luqman (Eds.), *Foundations of Islāmic Psychology: From Classical Scholars to Contemporary Thinkers*. Oxford: Routledge.

Rassool, G. H. (2023). Readiness for knowledge integration of Islāmic ethics and Islāmic psychology: An integrated research study. In G. H. Rassool (Ed.), *Advancing Islāmic Psychology Education: Model, Knowledge Integration, and Implementation*. Oxford: Routledge.

Rosenthal, F. (1970). *Knowledge Triumphant: The Concept of Knowledge in Medieval Islam* (pp. 46–69). Leiden: E. J. Brill.

Rosmarin, D. H. (2018). *Spirituality, Religion, and Cognitive-Behavioral Therapy*. New York: Guilford.

Schiler, J. (2003). Working with ICT: Perceptions of Australian principals. *Journal of Educational Administration*, 41(3), 171–185.

Schneider, M. (2012). Knowledge integration. In N. M. Seel (Eds.), *Encyclopedia of the Sciences of Learning*. Boston, MA: Springer.

Shaw, S., Cartwright, A., Spratley, T., & Harwin, J. (1978). *Responding to Drinking Problems*. London: Croom Helm.

Sherif, M. A. (1975). *Ghazālī's Theory of Virtue*. New York: State University of New York Press.

Skinner, N., Roche, A., Freeman, T., & Addy, D. (2005). Responding to alcohol and other drug issues: The effect of role adequacy and role legitimacy on motivation and satisfaction. *Drugs-Education Prevention and Policy*, 12(6), 449–463.

Sloan, R. P., Bagiella, E., & Powell, T. (1999). Religion, spirituality, and medicine. *Lancet*, 353, 664–667.

Sloan, R. P., Bagiella, E., & Powell, T. (2001). Without a prayer: Methodological problems, Integrating spirituality and psychotherapy ethical challenges, and misrepresentations in the study of religion, spirituality, and medicine. In T. G. Plante & A. C.

Sherman (Eds.), *Faith and Health: Psychological Perspectives* (pp. 339–354). New York: Guilford.

Tyler, T. R. (2006). Psychological perspectives on legitimacy and legitimation. *Annual Review of Psychology*, 57(1), 375–400.

Visser-Wijnveen, G. J., van der Rijst, R. M., & van Driel, J. H. (2016). A questionnaire to capture students' perceptions of research integration in their courses. *Higher Education*, 71(4), 473–488.

Wilson, S. (2001). What is an indigenous research methodology? *Canadian Journal of Native Education*, 25(2), 175–179.

Index

abduction 27
absolute 31, 70
AbuSulyman, A. H. 90, 101
academic 9, 18, 36, 54, 56, 66, 97
accommodate 7
accomplishments 4
accountability 43
accountable 22
acculturated 21, 29, 49
acquisition 1, 21, 87
actions 12, 22, 26, 42, 44, 76, 80
activities 8, 22, 73, 76, 77
adaptation 97, 98, 102
addictive 7, 18
addition 2, 21, 22, 28, 48, 51, 62, 68, 69, 95, 97–100
adherent 54
adolescent 98, 102
adoption 47, 90
advancement 20, 37
adversity 29
advocate 39
Ahmad 32, 33, 34, 36, 44, 45, 71, 101
akhlāq 28
al-Adaab 33
Al-Aĥzāb 87
al-Akhlāq 36
al-Albani 45, 82
al-Andalusi 34, 68, 71
Al-Anfal 38
al-aqliyah 31
Al-Baqarah 29, 31
Al-Bīrūnī 6
al-Bukhari 33, 70, 71
alcohol 103
Al-Fiqh 45
al-Fiqhiyyah 42
al-ghayb 32
Al-Ghazâlî 94

al-Haytham 6, 17, 29–33
Al-Ihsan 43
al-Islām 26
Al-Jibali 46, 82
Allāh 4, 22, 28–32, 38, 39, 64, 65, 67–69, 72, 73, 76, 80, 84, 85, 87, 88, 100
al-nafs 31
Al-Rahman 45
al-Rayḥān 6
Al-Rāzī 36, 46
Al-sabr 65
Al-Shafi 76
al-Shari'ah 41, 84
Al-Shatibi 3
al-tadabbur 77
alternative 13, 14, 17, 48, 54, 59
al-tibb 36
altruism 24
ambiguity 93
analogical 35
Andalusia 4
An-nafs 7, 18
an-Nawawi 46
anonymity 99
antagonistic 89
anthropological 3, 17
anxiety 9–11, 13, 14
apologism 48, 73, 74
apostle 76
application 7, 8, 18, 37, 41, 42, 46, 59, 62, 73, 76
appraisal 66
approval 31, 99
aql 31, 37, 39
aqli 21, 60, 90, 97
Arabia 34, 71, 82
architecture 88
ar-Raḥmān 6

Index

Ash-Shar'iah 76
assessment 7, 34, 81, 101
assistance 93
association 12, 13, 17, 19, 36, 37, 45, 46, 101, 103
assumptions 23, 24, 26, 48, 55, 97
atomistic 29
attitude 5, 30, 90–92, 99, 100, 102
attribution 68
Auda, J. 3, 17, 48, 54, 64, 65, 67, 72–75, 77, 79–82, 84, 88, 89
avoidance 43
awareness 21, 23, 44, 68, 75, 80
axiology 23, 54, 56

background 91, 93
Badri, M. 47, 57, 91, 101
barriers 92, 93, 99, 100
basic 2, 3, 31, 32, 36, 51, 64, 74, 78, 79, 81, 86, 94
behaviours 2, 7, 18, 29, 37, 50, 59, 69, 92–96, 98–100
beliefs 7, 8, 21, 23, 26, 30, 35, 52, 56, 73, 74, 80, 89, 92
Belmont-report 45
beneficence 36, 37, 43, 44
betray 73, 80
biases 2, 47–51, 53, 55
bias-focused 1
bi'l-ma'ruf 39
bioethics 35, 36, 45, 46
biological 92
biomedical 40, 41, 45, 46
blessings 32, 87
bottom-up 3
boundaries 23, 93
brain 57, 58
brainstorming 16
breathing 74
Bucaille, M. 23, 33
Buddhist's 74
Bukhari 42, 68, 71
burdens 43, 44
burgeoning 8

Caliphate 4
canon 49
capacity 44, 49, 61, 88, 91
capital 3, 4
captives 29
cartographies 57
categories 15, 39, 41, 43, 70, 73, 79, 80
categorisation 50

causation 92
centered 84
challenges 82, 103
Chamsi-Pasha, H. 37, 39, 45, 46
characterisation 32
charity 29
chemistry 6, 18, 88
Childress, J. F. 36, 37, 45
Christians 47
civilisation 7, 20, 22, 28, 33, 36, 46
classical 7, 8, 18, 20, 22, 36, 54, 56, 59, 61, 63, 65, 66, 73, 79, 88, 103
client-driven 2
clinical 7, 9, 13, 17, 19, 40, 41, 45, 46, 49, 51, 57, 89, 91
cognition 87
cognitive 9, 50, 102, 103
cognitive-behavioural 10
collaboration 50, 58
collectivism 24
colonialism 1, 49
colonisation 2, 19, 47, 48, 53, 54, 56, 58
commission 45
communication 69, 71, 102
comparison 6, 13, 81, 97
compassionate 23
competence 34, 63–65, 68, 69, 71, 76, 91
complementary 3, 22, 56, 88
compliance 30
comprehension 8, 65, 69, 81, 87
compromise 13
concept 17, 18, 28, 30, 32–35, 38, 41, 66, 68, 70, 71, 86, 87, 94, 97, 101, 103
conceptualisations 75
conclusion 1, 6, 16, 44, 50, 70, 81, 82
conditions 8, 10, 64
confidentiality 40, 44, 99
conflicts 41, 69
conformance 77
congruent 8, 21, 73, 80
connectivity 72
consciousness 24
consolidation 79
constructive 10, 51, 69, 77
construed 3, 30
consultation 93
consumers 4
contemplation 30
contemporary 8, 17, 18, 48, 54, 58, 59, 61, 66, 67, 73, 74, 82, 89, 103
context-based 35
contextual 11

Index 107

contradiction 22, 48, 73, 74
controversial 15
conundrum 8
conventional 13, 14, 77
correlational 15, 50
counselling 7, 8, 18, 37, 45, 67, 89
creation 32, 76, 80
cross-contextual 56
cross-cultural 45
cross-sectional 27
cultural 3, 8, 26, 33, 36, 37, 48, 53, 56, 57, 73
culturally 37
culture 24, 26, 35, 37, 53, 59, 71, 73, 92, 102
curriculum 8, 84, 86, 89–91, 93, 95, 96, 99, 101, 103
cycles 65, 66, 74, 75, 77, 78, 81, 82, 84, 86, 87, 95
cyclical 76

danger 67
Dar-alifta 17, 33, 34, 71
Darussalam 46, 57, 82
Dâwud 76, 82
death 64, 67
decades 8, 40, 50
deception 44
decolonial 58
decolonisation 47, 54, 56
decolonise 54, 58, 74
decolonising 54–58, 103
deconstruct 74
deconstruction 47, 91
deductive 3
deeds 35, 76, 87
definition 1, 34, 72, 77, 101
deliberation 31, 35
delineated 62
democratic 48, 50, 53
demographic 95, 97, 98
depressed 10
depression 10, 13, 14
depressive 9–11
derivation 28
designs 15
desires 38
develop 4, 8, 21, 38, 40, 56, 61, 62, 82, 101
development 1, 2, 7, 8, 12, 17, 32, 35, 38–40, 44, 47, 48, 53, 56, 59, 61, 65, 67, 81, 82, 84, 95, 101
deviant 68, 74

deviation 51
diagnosed 13
dialectical 38
dilemma 57, 101
dimensions 3, 37, 54, 59, 75–77, 82, 92
directional 14
disadvantaged 12
disagreements 69
disbelief 84
disciplines 7, 42, 47, 49, 60, 73, 77, 90, 100
disclosure 69
discourse 16, 20, 25, 32, 57, 72, 81
diseases 78
disorders 9–11
disposition 5, 97
dissemination 48, 51, 53, 67, 87
dissociated 49
distorted 52, 56
distress 38
divergent 62
diversity 18, 37
divorce 20
dominant 48, 54, 56
drinking 103
driving 11
drug 102, 103
dynamic 23, 31, 77

ecological 39, 63, 91
ecolonisation 47
economic 3, 36
ecumenicity 102
education 1, 8, 17–19, 33, 34, 36, 45, 55, 58, 70, 87, 90, 93, 100, 102–104
e-envisioning 45, 70, 82, 101
ego 74
elements 6, 10, 13, 29, 31, 34, 78–82, 86, 90
elimination 42, 46, 56, 73
embedded 1, 21, 35, 38, 66, 70, 87, 94, 103
embodiment 30
emergency 18
emotional 74, 101
emotions 26, 35, 92
empathy 38
empirical 5, 10, 21–24, 40, 59, 60, 65, 70, 90, 97, 99, 100
empiricism 65
employment 73
enlightened 4
enquiry 1, 77, 79

enterprise 49, 51
environment 4, 15, 32, 63, 81, 92
epistemic 56, 74
epistemicide 49
epistemological 8, 15, 19, 21, 23, 47–50, 56, 58, 59, 73, 90, 100, 103
epistemologies 2, 54, 82
epistemology 21, 23, 29, 31–33, 54, 56, 70, 90
equivalent 97
Esposito, J. 38, 45
establishment 56
ethical 14, 20, 22, 23, 26, 28, 29, 34–41, 43–46, 50, 53, 68, 69, 71, 90, 91, 93–97, 99–101, 103
ethnocentric 47
ethnocentrism 53
ethnography 15, 25, 27
etiquette 46
Eurocentric 1, 2, 47, 48, 54, 55, 59, 91
evaluation 13, 66, 67
evidence-based 13, 41, 53, 54, 58
evolution 8, 58
examination 5, 6, 10, 26, 36, 47, 54, 59, 66, 67
excellence 23, 31, 43
exclusion 50, 51, 89
exegesis 39, 67, 78, 87
existence 26, 28, 32, 38, 57
experimental 5, 15, 16, 31, 41, 50, 58, 101
exploitation 43
exploration 58, 78
exposure 13, 51, 52
extremists 64

facilitation 42
faculty 31, 37, 38, 97, 99
faith 5, 7, 17, 29, 42, 82, 85
fallacy 8
fashion 63, 72
feelings 35, 93
fertilisation 56
Fiqhiyyah 41
forbidden 8, 18
foreign 17, 33, 34, 71
formative 75, 81, 82, 84, 95
formula 23
formulation 10, 15, 19, 26
foundation 2, 21, 22, 33, 56, 73, 88, 103
foundational 24, 36
fragmentation 50, 73

framework 2, 8, 13, 15, 16, 19, 23, 24, 26, 37, 39, 46, 47, 59, 62, 63, 66–68, 70, 72, 75, 78–82, 84, 86, 91, 95, 96, 100
Freudian's 74
fundamental 2, 9, 20, 22, 26, 29, 32, 55, 65, 75, 80, 88, 97

generalisations 24
generation 2, 20
genocide 49
globalisation 1, 47–49, 53, 56, 58
God-consciousness 94
God-sociomoral 24
governance 37, 73
grassroot 8
group-based 97
groups 1, 12, 16, 78–82, 86, 97
growth 1, 47
guidance 38, 60, 77, 78, 84, 92
guidelines 36, 37, 40, 41, 45, 59, 63, 74
guiding 31, 64, 84, 90

habits 51
Hadith 33, 34, 57, 66, 70, 71, 82, 83
halal 38
handbook 102
happiness 100
harassment 39
hardship 39–42
hardwired 38
HARKing 51, 53, 57
harm 37, 39–44, 46
hazards 41
health 1, 7, 8, 13, 14, 17–19, 36, 44–46, 49, 53, 58, 63, 89, 102, 104
healthcare 35, 46, 102
health-related 36, 45
hearts 67, 77, 78, 80
hegemonic 57
heritage 4, 73
heuristic 25
hierarchy 66
highlight 16, 81
historical 2, 6, 7, 17, 20, 23, 32, 48, 61, 73
horizontal 62, 94, 103
human 5–7, 15, 18, 21–23, 25, 28, 31, 32, 35, 36, 38, 40, 42–46, 49, 50, 59, 60, 64, 69–71, 73, 80, 87, 101, 103
humanists 4

Index 109

humankind 38, 63
hypnotherapy 74
hypothesis 3, 6, 14–16, 32, 52, 62, 95
Ibn-Al-Haytham 5
Ibrāheem 85
identifying 9, 50, 66, 70, 80, 92
ideological 12, 49
ideologies 12, 55, 69, 80, 102
Ihsan 43
Ijtihad 61, 70
illuminate 3
imagination 30
imitation 48, 73, 74
immoral 42, 48
immune 21
impartial 63, 69
impediment 42
imperfection 5
implementation 14, 18, 44, 51, 90, 91, 94, 98–103
imposition 48, 49
inauthentic 68
inclusion 43, 51
incongruent 76, 88
incumbent 21, 65
independent 12, 32, 33, 61, 98
indigenous 19, 48, 49, 56–58, 104
individualism 24
individualistic 49
induction 3, 6, 27, 50, 81
inductive 3, 81
industrialised 50, 53
inferential 16, 50, 98
infertility 44
informal 53
information 1, 2, 10, 37, 38, 44, 52, 67, 68, 81, 99, 102
injunctions 4
innovation 90
insecurity 93
institution 32, 70
institutionalised 47
institutions 23, 36, 73
Insurgency 57
integrated 2, 3, 7, 8, 11–13, 17, 18, 24, 33, 53, 56, 59–62, 64, 70, 88–90, 96, 97, 103
integrity 37, 63, 68, 69
intelligence 38, 93, 101
intention 31, 39–42, 63, 65, 76, 80, 84, 85
interchangeably 26

interconnected 2, 3, 10, 22, 56, 72, 75, 84, 88, 93
interconnections 66, 72
intercultural 57
interdisciplinary 82, 101
interlinked 8
interpretation 5, 16, 29, 31, 38, 39, 48, 53, 67, 68, 70
interpretivism 26, 27
interrelationships 95
interventions 7–9, 13, 14, 42, 43, 51, 74
interwoven 50
introspection 48, 78
intuitive 5, 38
Islāmically 7, 9, 17
Islāmisation 59, 91, 99, 100
Islām-psychology 102

Jews 47
Judeo-Christian 24, 36
judgement 38, 41, 68, 87, 88
jurisprudence-logical 5
justice 36–38, 41, 43, 44, 46, 73, 84, 94

Kasule, O. H. 39–41, 46, 59, 100, 102
Kathir 39, 46, 78, 82, 87
Khaldun 6, 17, 34, 65, 71
kingdom 36
knowing 48, 49, 56, 87
knowledgeable 68, 92
knowledge-based 48

landscape 66, 89
language 1, 22, 26, 34, 64
law 32, 35, 41–44, 46, 76, 84, 88
lawful 67
leader 86, 87
leadership 50, 57, 88
learned 64, 67
learning 5, 34, 87, 90, 101, 103
legacy 57
legal 36, 41, 44, 46
legitimacy 84, 86, 89, 91–96, 98, 100, 103, 104
legitimate 92, 93
legitimation 104
libraries 4
licence 16
lifetime 4
limitations 9, 10, 16, 35, 47, 48, 53, 56, 62, 66, 72–74, 86, 97
lineage 76

110　Index

linear 63, 98
linguistics 22
literacy 102
literature 1, 7–10, 16, 54, 56, 63–67, 73–75, 79, 81, 84, 88–91
logic 75, 80
logical 8, 15, 22, 91
longitudinal 27, 53, 96
long-standing 2, 55
long-term 11
lunatic 44

magnitude 10
maintenance 41
majority 40, 91
makeup 92
malpractice 6
management 102
manifestations 32, 79
man-made 24
manuscripts 4
mapping 33, 63, 65, 66, 71, 86
Maqasid 8, 17, 45, 62, 64, 66, 70, 72–86, 95, 101
marriage 42
marshalled 54, 74
mastery 6, 65
materialistic 24
mathematics 4, 6, 88
maxims 41, 42, 44
meanings 3, 22, 24–26, 38, 63, 65–67, 74, 78, 80, 82, 86
measurable 10, 24
mechanism 46
medical 35–37, 45, 46, 101
medicine 4, 17, 18, 36, 43, 45, 46, 88, 102, 103
medieval 17, 18, 103
meditation 71
mental 1, 7, 17, 18, 25, 30, 32, 49, 87, 89, 100, 102
merciful 23
mercy 39
meta-analyses 9, 16
meta-analysis 16, 102
metaphysical 30, 32, 35
methodological 7, 8, 10, 27, 49, 50, 59, 66, 68, 72, 73, 78, 82, 97, 103
methods 2, 3, 10, 12, 15, 16, 22–25, 33, 34, 42, 52, 53, 59, 62, 65, 70, 82, 96, 99, 102
migration 42
mind–body 24
mind–body–soul 24
mindfulness 74
misconception 88
misinterpretation 51
misleading 48
misrepresentations 103
modalities 41
model 8, 16, 18, 19, 60, 86, 87, 90, 96, 97, 103
modernity 48, 57, 90
monetary 4
monocultural 1
monotheism 28
monotheistic 28, 29
moral 1, 20, 22, 26, 28, 29, 35–38, 43, 44, 50, 54, 59, 68, 86, 87, 90, 91, 93–95, 97–100, 102, 103
motivation 98, 103
motivational 93
multidisciplinary 61, 68
multimethod 27
Muslims 1, 7, 19, 22, 29, 35, 54, 58, 61, 70, 88, 89
mysticism 5
myths 18

nafs 7, 18, 35, 65
nafs-e-lawwāmah 74
nafs-e-muṭma'innah 74
narrations 64
narratives 8, 48, 97
Nasa'i 43, 45
naturalistic 24
nature 1, 3, 5, 7, 8, 11, 12, 14, 16, 22, 23, 26, 28, 31–33, 37, 38, 48, 55, 60, 63, 68, 77, 79, 86, 87, 89, 97
nectar 8, 18
negation 49
negative 13, 52, 80, 90, 97
neglected 22, 51, 57
network 17, 58
neutrality 15
niyyah 63, 76
non-Anglo-Saxon 1
non-directional 12, 14
non-Islāmic 79, 80, 88, 89
non-maleficence 36, 37, 43
non-malfeasance 37, 44
non-probability 15
non-White 1
normative 41, 55, 100
norms 100
notion 1, 21, 26, 38, 59, 72, 84, 87, 92

Index   111

novel 14
nuanced 73
null 14, 16, 51, 52

objectivity 23, 60
obligation 24, 40, 44, 93
observation 6, 16, 21, 31, 32, 60, 64
observational 52, 57
omissions 2, 55
one-tailed 14
onion 26
online 9, 46, 102
ontological 23, 47, 48, 56
ontologies 82
ontology 21, 23, 29, 30, 32, 33, 54, 56, 70
open-ended 12
operational 9, 100
opinions 41, 48, 54, 64, 65, 68, 73
oppositional 24
optics 5, 6, 30, 33, 88
optimism 51
organisational 15, 93, 96, 99, 100
organisation-driven 2
organisms 81
orientalism 56
orientation 21, 23, 24, 35, 56, 97
original 6, 42, 50, 68, 72, 73, 97
origins 20, 45
orphans 29
outcomes 1, 13, 14, 28, 43, 44, 52, 54, 62, 63, 74, 78
outline 53
outsourced 80
overarching 10
overruling 41
overview 2, 16, 36, 63, 72, 79, 88, 100

pandemic 40
paradigm 2, 21, 23–26, 28, 29, 32, 34, 36, 39, 48, 54, 55, 59–61, 69, 70, 87–90, 97
paradigms 12, 24, 33, 47, 100
parameters 26
parochial 24
partialism 48, 56, 73, 74
partialistic 74
patience 65, 87
patients 9, 10, 13, 14, 36
peer-reviewed 66
perception 6, 22, 23, 29–31, 50, 66, 77, 87, 89, 90, 92, 95, 96, 98, 100, 102
perceptualisation 79, 80
personal 16, 24, 35, 71, 92, 93, 96, 100

personality 68
perspectives 33, 35, 60, 76, 97, 103, 104
perversion 84
p-hacking 51, 53, 57
phenomena 2–4, 24
phenomenology 15, 25
philosophers 3–5
philosophical 8, 21, 23, 24, 26, 36, 56, 70
philosophies 25, 26, 55, 80
physical 4, 24, 28, 30, 32
physicians 3, 6, 19
physiological 30
pillar 38
pioneer 6, 29
plagiarised 69
plagiarism 44
plagiarisms 64
political 1, 8, 46, 47, 49, 56, 57
politics 73, 88, 102
polymaths 7
positivism 24, 26, 27
positivistic 89
positivist-quantitative 24
possession 7, 18, 87
post-colonial 47, 49
post-colonialism 1
post-graduate 101
post-modern 73
post-positivism 26
practitioner 43
pragmatism 25–27
prayer 29, 103
predictors 8, 84, 90, 92, 95, 96, 99, 103
predisposition 38
premature 51
premise 31
prerequisite 63
preservation 41, 73, 76, 85
presumption 30
prevention 42, 43, 92, 103
principle 35, 37, 39, 40, 42–44, 69, 87, 92, 94
probability 3, 15, 53
problems 1, 8, 10, 21, 50, 51, 55, 65, 68, 77, 98, 102, 103
problem-solving 8
procedures 6, 27, 59, 65, 99
processes 6, 21, 50, 59, 92, 100, 101
production 2, 19, 20, 48, 54, 56, 58, 69, 87, 91
professionals 92, 102
professions 81
proficiency 43, 65

progeny 41, 44, 76
prohibited 39, 40, 43, 44
prominence 68
promoting 4, 73
propagated 8
properties 52, 98, 102
propositions 66
protection 36, 37, 41, 44, 45, 69
psychiatric 44
psychiatry 46, 57, 89
psychological 3, 7, 36, 37, 42–45, 49–51, 57, 58, 76, 89, 101, 103, 104
psychologists 2, 37, 43–45, 47, 49, 53, 57, 61, 62, 65, 82, 92, 93, 101
psychometric 52, 98, 102
psychosocial 1, 8, 61
psychotherapeutic 8
psychotherapy 7, 8, 17–19, 21, 37, 45, 71, 82, 92, 103
puberty 44
purifying 22
purpose-driven 77
purposes 8, 41, 42, 44, 54, 55, 72, 74, 77, 80, 81
purposiveness 60

qualitative 2, 3, 11–13, 15–18, 24, 27, 33, 52, 59, 61, 62, 64, 66, 96
quantitative 2, 3, 5, 11–13, 15–18, 24, 27, 52, 53, 59, 61, 62, 64, 96
quasi-experimental 15
quasi-sacerdotal 29
question 8, 10–14, 17, 19, 23, 37, 43, 51, 52, 54, 59, 74, 76, 77, 92, 95
questionnaire 97, 98, 102, 104
questions 3, 5, 10–15, 50, 55, 56, 60, 65, 70, 81, 92, 95, 96, 101
Qur'ān 4, 20–24, 28, 35, 38, 39, 60, 61, 64–67, 69, 70, 74, 76–78, 80, 81, 84–87, 100, 101
Qur'ânic 5, 72

Rabaniyyah 32
randomising 51
Rassool, G. H. 7, 8, 18, 21, 29, 36, 38, 59–62, 71, 91, 100, 103
rational 5, 21, 22, 31, 38, 59, 60, 97
rationalism 22, 65
rationality 22, 32, 35, 100
reactions 13
readiness 91, 95, 96, 98–100, 102, 103
realism 25–27
reality 2, 20, 23–26, 28, 31, 32, 49, 54, 66, 67, 75, 79–82, 84, 88, 89

real-life 7, 63
reasoning 22, 31, 35, 37, 38, 48, 50, 61, 81
rebirth 7
reciprocating 42, 43
recollection 87
recommendations 16, 89
reconcile 90
reconsideration 2, 55
reconstructing 90
recourse 73
reductionism 50
redundant 42
re-envisioning 17, 82, 83
refinement 8, 36, 78, 81, 82
reflections 77, 78, 81, 82, 84, 86, 87, 95
reflexology 74
reform-oriented 100
regression 98
Reiki 74
reinforces 91, 93
relation 1, 15, 16, 22, 23, 35, 36, 39, 44, 67, 73, 91, 102
relationship 2, 13, 14, 23, 24, 28, 55, 89, 92, 93, 98
religion 7, 19, 23, 26, 32, 34, 35, 41, 42, 44, 46, 64, 76, 89, 101–103
Renaissance 3, 6, 36, 100
reorientation 70
re-oriented 65, 75
reproduced 47
reproducibility 50, 51, 58
researchers 1, 4, 13, 15, 19, 43, 44, 47, 48, 50, 51, 53, 54, 59, 64–66, 68, 74, 82, 97
resistance 57
resources 16, 35, 63, 76, 92, 103
restoration 31, 90
revelation 22, 24, 28, 31, 32, 37–39, 48, 56, 59, 70, 73, 74, 77, 79, 80, 82, 84, 87, 88, 90, 94, 100
revivalism 100
rhetoric 54
righteousness 28
robustness 62
role 7, 23, 31, 70, 75, 84, 86, 87, 89–96, 98–100, 102, 103
rubric 33, 70
rulings 63, 64

safeguards 43
Sahin 97, 98, 102
Sahin-Francis 102
salami-slicing 51
salutation 23

sample 12, 13, 15, 51, 53, 91, 97, 102
sampling 15, 50, 53, 65, 97, 102
schizophrenia 73
scholar 6, 20, 33, 67–70, 74, 77, 81
scholars 3–8, 18, 20–23, 30, 35, 36, 43,
 54, 56, 59, 61, 63, 65, 69, 72,
 75, 88, 103
scholarship 2–4, 7, 17, 20, 33, 34, 45,
 47–49, 54, 56, 59, 60, 65,
 69–75, 81–83, 101
scientific 3–6, 18–21, 23, 24, 28–33, 36,
 37, 40, 46, 54, 58, 59, 65, 70, 89
scrutinise 53
secular 21, 23, 24, 31, 47–49, 74, 82,
 90, 91
selection 44, 51, 52
selective 8, 29, 50, 52, 54, 77
self-citation 51
self-concepts 50
self-criticism 69
self-evident 38
self-help 9
self-interest 37
self-perception 92, 96, 101
self-reported 97
self-restraint 36
seminal 20, 74
sensations 25
sensory-cognitive 38
separation 35, 88
sequelae 49
sequential 62, 63, 86
Shari'at 44
significance 13, 20, 41, 50, 87
signs 21, 30, 80, 88
similarities 80
skills 21, 62, 65, 66, 68, 81, 93, 94, 99
sleep 44
socialisation 26
sociocultural 1, 3
socio-economic 64
sociology 57, 88
sociopolitical 1, 48, 87
solutions 2, 16
solution-specific 3
soul 7, 18, 19, 22, 31, 35, 38, 65, 76, 100
specialists 68
spirituality 7, 89, 91, 101–103
spiritual-structure 24
stages 8, 39, 44, 54, 74–76
statement 10, 32, 42, 64, 66, 67, 69, 77
statistical 16, 50, 54, 98
statistics 16, 59, 98
stepwise 19

structure 15, 23, 28, 40, 48, 90
styles 50
sub-disciplines 93
subjectivity 58
subpopulation 50
sub-principle 43
substance 98, 102
substance-using 103
Sufism 71
Sunnah 21, 22, 24, 28, 35, 67, 80, 94, 100
supremacy 48, 49
surgeons 19
suspects 5
symbolic 20
synthesis 16, 17, 60, 66, 90, 97
systematic 1, 8, 21, 67, 70, 72
systems 4, 37, 42, 44, 55, 73

tabulate 66
Tafsir 46, 64, 82
tanaqud 48
teacher-related 90
teaching-learning 99
techniques 4, 6–8, 15, 25, 27, 77
technology 22, 33, 58, 71, 90
temperance 94
tenets 80
terminologies 47
testing 3, 15, 16, 30, 62
textual 79
thematic 7, 16, 57
theologians 3
theology 5, 35
theory 1, 3, 6, 7, 10, 15, 16, 18, 21, 25,
 27, 32, 33, 44, 49, 65, 69, 71,
 74, 87, 90, 92, 93, 96, 101, 103
therapeutic 8, 43, 44, 74, 89, 101, 102
therapy–based 9
therapy-Islāmic 10
thinkers 8, 18, 59, 103
thought 4, 7, 20, 22, 26, 32–35, 45, 48,
 49, 54, 56, 58, 59, 65, 74, 76,
 80, 85, 88, 91, 100–103
time-bound 10
top-down 3
tradition 7, 18, 20, 21, 34, 35, 56
traditional 7, 17, 20, 33, 34, 71, 81, 82
traditions 17, 21–23, 35, 36, 59–61, 63,
 65, 69
transcultural 102
transformation 100
transparent 43, 51
triangulation 53
trilogy 32

trustworthiness 37
trustworthy 64, 68
two-tailed 14

umbrella 60, 90
unambiguous 42
unbiased 66
unconscious 48
underrepresentation 51
unethical 48
unicity 28–30
unintentionally 51
universal 31, 32, 35–37, 50, 72, 78–82, 86, 90
universally 37, 48
unlawful 67
unscholarly 69
urban 88
utilisation 7, 88, 89
utilise 7
utility 7
Utz 34

vaccine 40
validity 39, 40, 51–53, 63, 98
valuative 12
values 4, 21, 23, 24, 26, 28, 29, 31, 35, 48, 56, 59, 74, 78–82, 86, 89–100, 102, 103
variation 50
various 6, 14, 21, 22, 36, 54, 55, 60, 66, 90, 92, 100
version 14, 98

vertical 62, 86, 94, 103
viewpoint 30
violations 69
virtuous 39, 68
vision 17, 21, 26, 30, 33
visual 6, 50, 66
vulnerability 37

wa'l-Jamaa'ah 74
warranted 74
weaknesses 16
webbed 72, 79
websites 64
well-aligned 11
well-balanced 28
well-being 3, 43
well-built 19
well-versed 7
Westernised 49
Western-oriented 1, 29, 36, 48, 54
wholism 48, 72
wholistic 2, 3, 54, 74, 88, 89, 91, 95
widespread 47, 50
wisdom 6, 32, 94
withdraw 53, 99
withholding 44
worldview 2–5, 20, 21, 23, 24, 26, 28–30, 32–35, 47–49, 51, 54, 59, 65, 70, 72–75, 78, 80–82, 86, 88, 90, 92
worship 28, 76
worthwhile 21, 76
wrong-doing 84

For Product Safety Concerns and Information please contact our EU representative GPSR@taylorandfrancis.com
Taylor & Francis Verlag GmbH, Kaufingerstraße 24, 80331 München, Germany

www.ingramcontent.com/pod-product-compliance
Lightning Source LLC
Chambersburg PA
CBHW051753230426
43670CB00012B/2273